# Incredible Intervention

## LIVING LIFE IN THE MIRACLES OF GOD

### Christy Christopher

**BRIDGE LOGOS**

Newberry, FL 32669

**Bridge-Logos**
Newberry, FL 32669

**Incredible Intervention**
**Living Life in the Miracles of God**
by Christy Christopher

Printed in the United States of America

Library of Congress Catalog Card Number: 2018949490

International Standard Book Number: 978-1-61036-213-9

All Scripture quotations, unless otherwise indicated, are taken from the Holy Bible, New International Version®, NIV®. Copyright ©1973, 1978, 1984, 2011 by Biblica, Inc.॥ Used by permission of Zondervan. All rights reserved worldwide. www.zondervan.com The "NIV" and "New International Version" are trademarks registered in the United States Patent and Trademark Office by Biblica, Inc.॥

Scripture quotation marked (NLT) are from the Holy Bible, New Living Translation ®, copyright © 1996, 2004 by Tyndale Charitable Trust. Used by permission of Tyndale House Publishers. All rights reserved.

Scripture quotation marked "PHILLIPS" are from The New Testament in Modern English by J.B Phillips copyright © 1960, 1972 J. B. Phillips. Administered by The Archbishops' Council of the Church of England. Used by Permission.

Scripture quotation marked "KJV" are from King James Version Public Domain.

Scripture quotation marked "NKJV" are from Scripture taken from the New King James Version®. Copyright © 1982 by Thomas Nelson. Used by permission. All rights reserved.

Scripture quotation marked "AMPC" are from The Amplified Bible, Classic Edition Copyright © 1954, 1958, 1962, 1964, 1965, 1987 by The Lockman Foundation.

Scripture quotation marked "ESV" are from the English Standard Version The Holy Bible, English Standard Version. ESV® Text Edition: 2016. Copyright © 2001 by Crossway Bibles, a publishing ministry of Good News Publishers.

Scripture quotation marked "MSG" are from The Message Copyright © 1993, 1994, 1995, 1996, 2000, 2001, 2002 by Eugene H. Peterson

Scripture quotations marked NASB New American Standard Bible® (NASB), Copyright © 1960, 1962, 1963, 1968, 1971, 1972, 1973, 1975, 1977, 1995 by The Lockman Foundation. Used by permission. www.Lockman.org.

All Hebrew and Greek definitions derived from
http://www.eliyah.com/lexicon.html

Cover/Interior design by Kent Jensen | knail.com

# ENDORSEMENTS

Christy is a gift from God not only to our local church fellowship but also to the entire body of Christ. I am fortunate enough to witness God using Christy on a weekly basis ministering to people in our church through prophetic words of encouragement. Every time she speaks publicly on behalf of the Holy Spirit, I can always confidently receive her words as being from the Lord both in content and in timing. This book is an expression of her intimate relationship with God as she invites the reader to embrace the Father's love and ever-abounding grace. You will be sure to receive a powerful gift of hunger for God's word and presence that will only be satisfied with time well spent with Him!

**—BRYAN FINLEY**, SENIOR LEADER, HOPE CHAPEL, APEX, NORTH CAROLINA, BRYANFINLEY.COM

Christy and I have been dear friends for over thirty-seven years, and over those years I have watched her pursue the Lord with all her heart through many great difficulties. As you open her book, she will take you back through the years, recounting in detail each of those incredible moments in which God left His indelible handprint of divine intervention on her difficult and, at times, seemingly impossible circumstances. Christy's passionate desire is that all of these stories will serve to encourage you, her beloved reader, that the Lord's hand is just as powerful in your life as He has proven himself to be in hers, and as a result, you will be encouraged to entrust yourself to Him as you encounter difficult or impossible circumstances in your own life.

**—TAMI HULSE**, MINISTRY LEADER, ABUNDANT LIFE FELLOWSHIP, MT. GILEAD, OHIO

*Incredible Intervention* is the story of God's marvelous intervention in the Christophers' lives. What Christy and Nathan have *"seen with [their] eyes, which [they] have looked at and [their] hands have touched"* (1 John 1:1) is what Christy proclaims in this book. The reading of it will pull you in and build your own faith at every turn. No weak hearsay evidence, this—this is the real eyewitness stuff. Enjoy!

—**MICHAEL A. COTTEN**, ANTIOCH INTERNATIONAL MINISTRIES, JAMESTOWN, NORTH CAROLINA

Christy's book, *Incredible Intervention*, reveals in a captivating and beautiful way the testimony of Jesus intervening in the lives of those He loves. This book gives voice to the deep and intentional love of the Father for us as His children and points the way to all that is available to us in Christ Jesus. You will be encouraged and strengthened as you read testimony after testimony of God's kindness, faithfulness, provision, and love for His children. Each story and testimony becomes an invitation to us, the readers, to step into that same place and experience Jesus in that same way in our own lives. There is so much more in Christ for us to know and encounter, and He is waiting for us to grab His hand and allow Him to lead us on an adventure into "Incredible Intervention."

—**DANEEN BOTTLER**, TY AND DANEEN BOTTLER MINISTRIES, PORTLAND, OREGON, WWW.TYANDDANEENBOTTLER.COM

While reading *Incredible Intervention*, I was captivated by each and every personal story shared. There were many that I could directly relate to. But more to my surprise, it gently prompted self-reflection on how the ordinary, mundane parts of life can be anything but . . . if we have eyes to see the hand of the Father at work.

—**REBEKAH TOZER**, WELLNESS COACH, APEX, NORTH CAROLINA

Nathan and Christy are not special. They are ordinary people living an extraordinary life in Christ. If they *were* special, then these stories would be merely stories that only happen to "special" people. But these stories are far from that! They will call you higher to live and walk in a belief that God is good and cares about your every need. These stories will give you the courage to say "I can trust God and wait on Him, because if He did it for them He can do it for me!" No, they are not special—they are extraordinary!

—**REBECCA DEVORE**, ARTIST/ILLUSTRATOR,
PORT HUENEME, CALIFORNIA

There are few people today who I can say are wholeheartedly sold out to Jesus and live their lives in constant communion with Him—living a life of dependence on Jesus. Christy is one of those rare treasures. The marvelous provision of Jesus is for us all, not just Christy and Nathan. I can attest to many of these amazing testimonies, and every time, it was an encouragement to me to dream *BIG* and trust in my *amazing* God! I'm excited to have your faith grow as you read and personally experience God's miraculous grace in your own life. I trust that you will in turn share your testimony—triumphing *"by the blood of the Lamb and by the word of [your] testimony"* (Revelation 12:11 KJV).

—**LINDA S. HOEFLICH**, RETIRED PRINCIPAL,
MANSFIELD CHRISTIAN SCHOOL, MANSFIELD, OHIO

In Matthew 5:16, Jesus says, *"Let your light shine before others, that they may see your good deeds and glorify your Father in heaven."* I can't think of a better way to describe Christy and the heart that she has for others. I have had the pleasure of working with her, and I have personally witnessed her pouring into people and standing in the gap for those in need. Her devotional messages are a testimony to *God-stories* in her day-to-day life. She helps readers identify and realize God's hand in their personal journeys. You will be blessed!

—**JULIE CUMMINS**, DIRECTOR, MARION COUNTY BOARD OF DEVELOPMENTAL DISABILITIES, MARION, OHIO

Christy Christopher has done it again. She has written another book full of inspiration, full of hope, and full of love for God. Her first book, *Until the Day Breaks and the Shadows Flee*, was just as engaging as *Incredible Intervention*. It is so very evident that the Holy Spirit works through her—all the way onto the pages of her books. The words flow and fill the reader with knowledge and wisdom, and in this book you will see how the wonders of God have continuously led Christy and her husband to want nothing more than to have a relationship with Him. "The supernatural is our normal," Christy Christopher says, and the miracles and wonders that God has and continues to perform in her life challenge the reader to note the wonders of God in their own. I most certainly have and do!

—**SHELLY MORROW WHITENBURG**, AUTHOR, CYPRESS, TEXAS

All Bible-believing Christians agree that the Holy Spirit's work of bringing people to a saving knowledge of Jesus is supernatural. When it comes to the issue of the supernatural being a part of the average Christian's everyday life, however, evangelicals—particularly in the western world—continue to be divided. Stories like the ones that Christy shares in this book are hard to argue with though! In the pages that follow, you will find ample evidence of God's miraculous intervention in day-to-day circumstances, as well as a practical, helpful explanation of God's empowering work from a traditional Charismatic perspective. Regardless of where you fall on issues such as the "baptism of the Holy Spirit" and the continuation of spiritual gifts in the post-apostolic age, the experiences Christy shares from her family's life will inspire you and build your confidence that God sees you, loves you, and is ready to work in all the events of your life, both big and small!

—**JEFF CHRISTENSEN**, PASTOR AND THEOLOGY INSTRUCTOR,
FAYETTEVILLE, NORTH CAROLINA

"Pure Delight" are the words that come to my mind as I read these personal stories of remembrance of God's provision and goodness poured out upon His people. These accounts of the faithfulness of God's presence among us are sure to strengthen your faith, as they have mine.

—**ERICA RUSSELL**, ARTIST, SPEAKER, TEACHER, MANSFIELD, OHIO

Christy's life and this book are so important in this day and age. Knowing Christy for many years, I know that she is a disciple who loves Christ with all her heart, mind, soul, and strength. This book will challenge you to put God's Scriptures over your personal feelings and preferences. This is an account of Christy's life calling each of us to live an all-or-nothing life with Christ, surrendered completely to His leadership. God doesn't want to be *part* of our lives and only called upon in our moment of need. No, His love, grace, mercy, forgiveness, and miracles bring a compelling to yield all!

—**TODD ROESE**, LONG-TERM MISSIONARY IN RUSSIA,
WESTERVILLE, OHIO

Christy has a passion for the Word of God. She pursues His truth, His power, and His very essence with a zeal and hunger unlike anyone I know. Christy has experienced God's deliverance, His restoration, His faithfulness, and His unrelenting love during hardships. She has been to the *Secret Place* of God, and she writes, teaches, and lives from that secret place. Christy's words will lead you into a greater desire to walk in God's presence and experience His love as well. Her writings will take you with her to the secret place of the Most High.

—**MELISSA G. BOLDEN**, INTERNATIONAL AUTHOR/SPEAKER, HOLLY SPRINGS, NORTH CAROLINA, WWW.MBOLDENMINISTRIES.COM

# DEDICATION

This book is dedicated to our seven grandchildren, any more grandchildren God adds to our family, and all the generations to come.

*Rhys Andrew / Lucy Annabelle*

*Eleanor Lois / Thomas Nathan / Ava Josephine*

*Rodney Jquell III / Remington Vera*

You were put on this earth for a great purpose. You were sent into our family so we may nurture, steward, and prepare you for life. You are arrows in our family quiver being made ready for your launch into the earth. You have a special voice. You have a unique personality to reflect the character and nature of God.

As you grow and learn to read, may this book of God-stories from your Mimi and Pappy help you to see just how God loves us and wants to be intimately involved in every detail of our lives. May the words on these pages help you to see how you, too, can participate in the miracles, signs, and wonders of God, who is bursting to love His world in so many tangible ways.

> *One generation shall commend your works to another, and shall declare your mighty acts.* (Psalm 145:4 ESV)

> *It has seemed good to me to declare the signs and wonders which the Most High God has done for me. How great are His signs and how mighty are His wonders! His kingdom is an everlasting kingdom And His dominion is from generation to generation.* (Daniel 4:2-3 AMP)

# CONTENTS

## PART ONE

# THE BRIDGE

## PART TWO

# FOREWORD

Everyone needs a friend like Christy Christopher. If you had the opportunity to spend just two minutes in her presence, your faith would be strengthened, your hope restored, and your prayer life invigorated. I know. She has been my friend for nearly twenty-five years.

I have observed Christy on the mountaintop of victory and in the valley of disappointment. In both places, her faith has been resilient, and her joy has been contagious. Oh! How I wish you could spend just five minutes with her!

But the good news is that you can! You can spend time with my dear friend, Christy Christopher! You can get to know Christy's heart, her life, and her faith through her new book, *Incredible Intervention*.

The Bible says, *"And they overcame him by the blood of the Lamb, and by the word of their testimony, and they loved not their lives unto the death"* (Revelation 12:11).

This Scripture gives the believer a clear and concise way to overcome any situation, event, or circumstance that has come against you to defeat you. You overcome by the blood of Jesus Christ and by *the word* of your *testimony*. The word "testimony" in this verse is really just an old-fashioned word for what our generation calls *story* or *narrative*.

I love this Scripture because it reminds me every time I read it that my story matters to God! The things that I have experienced in life, the prayers that have been answered, and the miracles that have lined my pathway are all an intrinsic part of my victory in Christ.

Christy's story matters. And so does yours!

There is something about a miracle—large or small—that just captures one's attention, doesn't it? Whenever God answers a desperate prayer in an unbelievable fashion, we all stop and stare. We all celebrate yet shake our heads nearly in disbelief. Christy's book spurs me on to expect the unexpected and to believe for the unbelievable.

As you read Christy's incredible yet ordinary stories, you will see the fingerprint of God on every page. You will know that the God of Moses, of Abraham, and of Daniel is still working in the lives of His children today. You will know that what God did for Peter, for Paul, and for Lazarus, He can still do for you! We serve a mighty God of wonders and miracles! He is still divinely and powerfully working in the lives of His children.

I think as you read the pages contained between the covers of this book that a sweet ache will begin to grow in you for the miraculous to become a part of your daily experience. You will thirst for the uncommon miracles that Christy's common life has welcomed. And when you have read the last page, you will be completely satisfied—yet you will be left longing for so much more! You, like me, will pine for greater miracles in your everyday life.

When my children were little, we used to sing a song that went like this:

"I anticipate the inevitable, supernatural, intervention of God—I expect a miracle!"

Do you? Do you anticipate the inevitable, supernatural, intervention of God? I believe that after reading this book you will! You will indeed anticipate God's incredible intervention in your ordinary life.

And while I'm at it, let me just say, "You're welcome!"

You're welcome. It has been my pleasure to introduce you to my powerful friend, Christy. In case I haven't mentioned before, we all need a friend like her. And now she is your friend as well!

With joy
—Carol McLeod
http://carolmcleodministries.com

# THE INVITATION

The cross and resurrection of Jesus Christ
is the greatest rescue mission of all time.

You know, we're just regular people looking and searching for the meaning of life. Why were we born? What is my purpose? Many times I don't have answers for some of life's probing questions, but this one answer I do have: *Jesus.*

You were born to have fellowship with God. You were born to love and be loved by God.

Sin has separated us from God. Jesus was sent by the Father, took our punishment on the cross, and cleared the way for us to have a relationship with God. The only thing we have to do to gain that relationship is believe in Jesus Christ and His work on the cross—and follow Him. You must repent of your sins and allow the blood of Jesus to wash over you, cleansing you from all unrighteousness. And *repent* simply means to turn or change your way of thinking.

Dear reader, if you have never surrendered your life to Jesus Christ and had a *soul-conversion*, I am praying for you now. You are so loved by the God of this universe! He is calling you and drawing you this very moment. He is asking you to turn around and come into the power of His love and desire for you.

God does not ask you to be perfect before you can form a relationship with Him. Out of our union with Jesus Christ comes empowerment to be who He created us to be. He is calling you to absorb His stringless love.[1] He is extending an invitation for you to become the you He had in mind the first time He thought of you. He desires to talk to you. He desires to walk with you. He desires to show you sights and take you on incomparable adventures.

You were created to fit perfectly in God's heart. Consider surrendering your confusing, chaotic life to Him. No, all will not automatically be a bed of roses when you do, but you will experience God, who gives you everything you will need for this life and godliness. (See 1 Peter 1:3.) You will find joy when sadness should prevail. You will encounter hope when there is a natural reason to stop hoping. You will experience cleansing of your soul no matter what dark deed you have done.

It's simple—God loves you and desires to spend eternity with you.

Love brings choice. He will not force or coerce. He simply extends an invitation. He desires your friendship. What you do with Jesus will determine your destiny. It will also determine your whole eternity-life beyond earthly living.

If you wish to make this *life-change* now, just tell Him. Tell Jesus you are sorry for how you have lived your life. Ask Him to cleanse you of all sins. Tell Him you want to follow Him and do what He tells you to do from this day forward. Ask Him to fill you with His love. Breathe deeply, and let the rivers of living water wash over you. It's a new day. He will come and make His home with you now. As you confess Jesus Christ as Lord, your eternal address will be changed to heaven.

When we become a Christian, the Holy Spirit moves in, and we become a temple of the Holy Spirit. (See 1 Corinthians 6:19.)

---

1   God's love is stringless in that He loves us even if we don't love Him. He laid down His life for us *while we were still sinners* (Romans 5:8). Yet we will never be able to fully absorb and enjoy His love for us until we discover His love and enter a faith-relationship with Him.

If you just asked Jesus to be Lord of your life, congratulations! Welcome to the family of God. You are now a temple of the Holy Spirit.

In the words of Kris Vallotton, Senior Associate Leader of Bethel Church, "The Son of God came as a man so men could become the sons of God."

.

> *For God so loved the world, that He gave His only begotten Son, that whoever believes in Him shall not perish, but have eternal life. For God did not send the Son into the world to judge the world, but that the world might be saved through Him.*
> (John 3:16-17 NKJV)

> *For you are all sons of God through faith in Christ Jesus.*
> (Galatians 3:26 NKJV)

# INTRODUCTION

If it's impossible to please God without faith, then it's
logical to conclude I will regularly find myself in places where
my faith must be engaged. We utterly need to pray
every day, "Be thou my vision."

This book isn't for the lukewarm. This book has the potential to
catapult you into new places and spaces with God you didn't know
existed. The stories are true. I simply cannot stay quiet any longer.

I want to first share with you a word of encouragement a
friend gave me concerning this book months before I even began
the first *stroke of the pen.*

I literally see this book dripping with the glory of God.
Every testimony and grace you write about in there, you
release empowerment for the same grace to be released,
whether it's physical healing or in marriage, financial . . .
whatever it is you testify of in this book, every person who
reads it will be affected by the glory of God in whatever
area they have need.

I'm seeing it is like where water runs to the lowest part
of the cavern—whatever the need is, it will draw it from
this book. It will literally be alive and anointed like the
Word of God. Whatever is needed, they will draw from
it. There will not even be anyone who picks up the book,
not even the ones who put it together, who publish it—
anybody who in any way has any contact of any type with
this book—[who] will [not] be affected by the glory of

God. And they will never be the same.

It's very powerful. It has been written on the timeline of God. It will only be done when He says it's done, because it's been written. You will know. As you begin to write this, there will be such a grace on it. You will be so compelled and so moved from the depths of your being to do it. The moments you are releasing this seed, everything else will fade into the background because you will be so compelled and inspired of the Spirit to release it onto the page.

The Scripture I'm getting to confirm [this] is Revelation 19:10. *"For it is the Spirit of prophecy who bears testimony to Jesus."* As you testify of what Jesus has done in your life, it will literally prophesy to those who partake in the pages."

—Lorena Hill

I never want to come across as a know-it-all. Sometimes you pray your heart out, and things still don't change. What should you do when that happens? You should continue trusting and praying in the face of perceived defeat. Remember, you are still growing, and there's still so much to learn and discover.

What shouldn't you do? You shouldn't get bitter and quit praying and trusting. There's a whole spiritual, dark realm out there that wants to take you down! But there's also a God who loves you and will take you into His loving embrace in the face of pain and heartache.

Go higher. May your adversary be shamed as he has to watch you draw near to God in the face of adversity and disappointment.

This book simply contains testimonies of what God has done. I have no formula or magic wand to ensure that every time I pray I will get the answer I want. There is still mystery and much to comprehend. But one thing I know: God is good, and the devil is a liar.

I am here on earth contending for my faith and growing in the knowledge of His will and purpose for me. Sometimes I hit the mark, and sometimes I don't. But no matter the outcome of my prayers, I have learned to continue in trust and devotion to Christ, who gave His life for me so I could have life.

Think about a circumstance you are facing right now that feels or seems insurmountable or overwhelming. Maybe it's a place in your heart that won't stop bleeding. Maybe it's a financial difficulty or marriage trouble. Possibly it's a child who has become frustrating to a parent. There might be an illness plaguing your body. If you are willing, right now, ask the Holy Spirit to meet you in this place as your read our story.

Ask God to open the eyes of your heart concerning the mountain you are facing.

Maybe you have plateaued in your spiritual journey, and there are no giants or mountains in front of you at the moment, but you are simply hungry for more. Tell God. Whatever your place in life, I believe God put this book into your hands for His purposes. It's my prayer that He will open the eyes of your heart and take you on a journey of more dimensions and experiences of His love and intentions for you. I pray He will give you fresh direction, correction, and revelation of His heart and will for your life.

We utterly need to pray every day, "Be thou my vision."[2]

Without heavenly vision, we are spiritually handicapped and impaired. Spiritual impairment simply means that we are

---

2   *Be Thou My Vision*—a traditional Irish Christian hymn often attributed to Saint Dallán Forgaill. The bestknown English version, with some minor variations, was translated by Eleanor Hull and published in 1912. https://en.wikipedia.org/wiki/Be_Thou_My_Vision

making decisions and perceiving what is happening based on earthly vision and unreliable emotions instead of putting on the *lens of faith* to enable us to see how things really are and correctly process what is happening.

It is a terrible thing to see and have no vision.[3]

—Helen Keller

God is about to modify your vision and alter your perspective! When the natural realm appears larger than God to you, it is sure proof you aren't using the lens of faith. It is my prayer that you will exit the reading of this book more heavenly minded than when you opened the first page. It's my prayer to spur you on to ask more questions and study His Word more intensely.

If you need to repent, then repent. If you need to rededicate your life to Jesus, then do so. If you need to receive Jesus Christ as your Savior for the very first time, then please do. Wherever you are, He is here for you to pull you onto His lap and love and care for you in ways that will refresh your soul to the core of your being. He is ready and waiting to use you as His ambassador in the earth for such a time as this.

I encourage you to read 2 Kings 6:8-23 in *The Message* version of the Bible. Remember, when you are walking upon the ancient pathways of God, you may see things others cannot see. It's always wrong to come to any conclusion based on what you see with your natural eye only. I heard Graham Cooke (popular speaker/author and owner of Brilliant Book House) say one time, "Our circumstances are not the problem! It's our perception of our circumstances that is the problem."

I love quotes. Here's one more quote by Helen Keller:

---

3    Attributed to Hellen Keller on Brainy Quote, https://www.brainyquote. com/quotes/helen_keller_165500

Although the world is full of suffering, it is also full of the overcoming of it.[4]

In my first book, *Until the Day Breaks and the Shadows Flee*, I shared a devotional trilogy about lessons in faith, hope, and love. Several people have said they would love to hear my story. Others have asked me about what I went through to enable me to share such material and encouragement from the Lord. I never really knew how to answer them, because I could never think of a single difficult season or turbulent event that caused me to write my first book.

It wasn't until the week I began writing this book when the Holy Spirit quickened to me that my first book was born out of what I am writing in this, my second book. I am pleased to say that I am now sharing the story others have asked for. The places my husband and I have traveled with God will astound you. I have no doubt.

My husband Nathan and I stand on the threshold of having experienced thirty-seven years of miracles, signs, and wonders together as I begin this book. I heard someone say one time that God will sometimes put a *Goliath* in your life to allow you to find the *David* within. It is time to tell the world.

We are overwhelmed each time another otherworldly event comes crashing in on us. It happens regularly. It comes in like the feel of a shooting star that I happen to catch suddenly and most unexpectedly. Each is a clarion call to notice how intimately I am cocooned into the lining of God's heart for me. I am situated in the loving palm of His hand. No one can pluck me out of the epicenter of His loving embrace!

Some folks have trials in health. Others seem to face times of injury and accidents. For other people there are cycles of testing

---

4    Attributed to Hellen Keller on Brainy Quote, https://www.brainyquote.com/quotes/helen_keller_109208

in other ways. Many, like my husband and me, have had regular times of testing in our finances.

We are regular tithers and givers. We are also regular participants in miraculous provision.

Financial miracles have been abundant. In our thirty-seven years of marriage we have experienced receiving unexpected checks, debt cancellations, money appearing in peculiar spots, and many other signs and wonders. This book contains an accounting of many of those stories coupled with spiritual encouragement and Scripture studies of lives lived in the Holy Spirit.

We as faithful Christians still have moments in our lives of weakness, discouragement, and faithlessness. Isn't it wonderful that when we are faithless He remains faithful?[5]

Regularly, God has told us (in our frailty and stumbling) to put on the lens of faith, the lens of hope, or the lens of love. God will fill us with sight if we allow Him to. I'm not speaking of what we can see with our natural eyes. Did you know there is a whole world around you that you cannot see with your natural eye? By putting on the correct lens of the Holy Spirit, life will go from black and white to Technicolor.

The ebb and flow of spiritual activity has catapulted us into a state of wordless wonder countless times!

So we give to you what has been given to us: stories of our miracles, signs, and wonders—events that could have only been created by the hand of a loving God who pines to lavish upon His children daily. We give to you a fresh dimension of wordless wonder as you walk through the pages of this book.

Experiencing God's intervention is to be part of the normal Christian life. If your walk with God is boring, you are 100% responsible. If we live the life God intended for us, there will be no earthly adventure that will compare. There is no room for

---

5 "If we are faithless, he remains faithful, for he cannot disown himself" (2 Timothy 2:13).

yawning and boredom in the Kingdom of God.

In Nathan's words:

This is the story of the stories of our life. All of the events are true—all told as my memory recalls. As I remember these adventures, I am quickly reminded that my life was only held on course by God's goodness and favor toward us.

My time on earth thus far has never seemed to bring me great wealth as far as money is concerned. On the other hand, what a wealth of God's love I have seen! God's blessing is better than a bird in the hand or two birds in the bush. It's more sure than any amount of money in the bank.

God saved my personal soul once, but He has saved our lives over and over again. Even as I write this, my eyes fill with tears just remembering it all.

At the end of each chapter in this book I have inserted what I call, *God whispers*. You might ask, "What are 'God whispers?'"

The whispers from God that I offer are what I believe God wants to speak to us at the end of the chapters as we complete them. With the *whispers*, I am speaking to you on behalf of God.

"But can someone really speak on behalf of God?" you might ask. The answer is most certainly, yes.

Paul wrote, "But the one who prophesies speaks to people for their strengthening, encouragement and comfort."[6]

The word translated "prophesies" in the Greek simply means to speak forth by divine inspiration. You and I can be divinely inspired to speak on behalf of God for the purpose of strengthening, encouraging, and comforting. Such speaking

---

6    1 Corinthians 14:3.

never replaces the written Word, of course, and it must always line up with the heart of what God says in the Bible.

I realize there are many *crazies* out there, and some people may count me in their number, but that's okay. I'm willing to take the criticism. The Scriptures and the Lord will be my judge if I misspeak in my attempt to relay to you what I believe God has given to me. I remain open to critique, and if anyone can show me an error in my writings by pointing to Scripture, I am open to hearing as I continue to grow in my relationship to Christ.

Dick Eastman, President of Every Home for Christ, said, "Only those who see the invisible can attempt the impossible."

So go with us now on our adventures in the Holy Spirit. Let God amaze you and bring fresh wonder into your soul! We promise you will walk away hungry for more!

> *Thus says the LORD: "Stand by the roads, and look, and ask for the ancient paths, where the good way is; and walk in it, and find rest for your souls."* (Jeremiah 6:16a ESV)

> *What you're after is truth from the inside out. Enter me, then; conceive a new, true life.* (Psalm 51:6 MSG)

## GOD'S WHISPER

Yes, ask me, dear one. Ask for those ancient pathways. Ask for the pathway through the sea of trouble. Investigate my activities. Become a student of my thoughts and intentions for you. My Word is full of how I deal with those in trouble and hardship. Ask me questions, and let me instruct you. Allow me to bring you to the plumb line of why you exist and the glory I put in you as you reflect me in the earth. Ask me to expand you into all I have planned and prepared for you. I need your *Yes* as we travel forward toward your heavenly destination. On this road, there is great beauty and grandeur to witness. There are great obstacles to overcome. There are unbelievers to witness to by your words and lifestyle. I call you to create hunger in others. I touch you so you may touch others. There is more. There is a surplus of activities in the spiritual realm for you to understand and walk out. The best place of rest is in the center of my glorious activities. Enter in. Open up and absorb my straight-line agape love for you. Your best days are still in front of you.

# Part One

# Money Under Our Door

What I see through the lens of truth—God's Word—often contradicts what I can see and feel with my natural senses. What I see looking at life through the lens of a lie—a word or thought that contradicts God's Word—often agrees with what I am experiencing and feeling in my emotions.

When Nathan asked my dad for permission to marry me, he told my dad that he offered to me what God had promised to us. That promise included that God would provide for us and never leave or forsake us. Nathan told Dad I was okay with that. My dad, a man of faith himself, gave Nathan his blessing.

Nathan wasn't even employed at the time. Faith or foolishness, we were stepping forward into the unknown world of adulthood with hardly a dime in our pocket—but full of hope for a great life together!

The first year of our marriage was a bit tumultuous. We were simply two twenty-year-old kids in love living on a shoe-string budget. Our combined incomes totalled $2,300 in our first year of marriage. And I became pregnant with our first child three months into our marriage.

We were on our way to my parents for Sunday dinner on a particular Sunday afternoon. I was about six months pregnant. We were traveling down a snowy country road when we crested a hill just in time to *T-bone* the side of a car just pulling out of a drive. I was fine, but Nathan hit his head on the windshield.

It wasn't until a week later, while Nathan was sitting in church, when the top half of his vision began to go black in one eye. We knew that couldn't be good, of course. And after getting his eye checked, he was rushed into emergency surgery for the repair of a detached retina.

That was a frightening experience for two kids newly married and with a child on the way. We had no health insurance, but the insurance of the man whose car we hit covered all medical expenses, praise God! The surgery was a success. The doctor told us Nathan would be in the hospital for eight to ten days and off work six to ten weeks. That was certainly not in our budget.

But God had other plans!

After just two days in the hospital, the doctor informed us Nathan was healing faster than anything he had ever seen and could go home. A day or two later the doctor told us Nathan could go back to work hanging drywall.

His eye was completely healed just ten days after surgery. It was a miraculous healing.

Even with the miraculous healing, though, Nathan still missed some work, and we were quickly gathering a pile of bills. Nathan didn't even know the total of our debts, because—feeling so overwhelmed—he was afraid to add everything up. We prayed and asked God to help us.

One night we came home to find an envelope under our apartment door. Inside was a cashier's check for what seemed like the random amount of $1,087.13. At the time, that was close to half a year's wages for us. We were dumbfounded! The note with the check said, "This is an odd amount, but it's what we felt the Lord told us to give you, so use it prayerfully."

Nathan quickly gathered our bills and started adding them up. To the penny, our bills came to—you guessed it—$1,087.13!

In a small season of crisis, our God showed off by, first, covering all of our medical expenses, then by giving Nathan an accelerated, doctor-mind-blowing healing, and then finally, by paying off all of our bills through some obedient God-fearing soul.

This first major, miraculous provision would lay the foundation for countless ways God would take care of *His kids*.

*I will give thanks to the Lord with my whole heart; I will recount all of your wonderful deeds.* (Psalm 9:1 ESV)

## GOD'S WHISPER

You are in the palm of my hand. I see when you go out, and I see when you stay in. My love is running all around you and within. The wind is my breath of desire for you. The oceans are but a drop of my affections toward you. I come and blow upon your circumstances at times with waves of my love and care for you. At times I hold back so you may be stretched and matured, but then it is my joy to come running in with fresh supplies from my heart to yours. When I watch you arise in courage and strength,

I am glorified again. I know you would rather not walk in the high waters of life. I understand you would prefer to stay out of the flames. Listen, dear one, and I will tell you it is in the flood when you are formed. It is in the fire where purification comes. Trust me. Trust me. Believe me. The strenuous, rugged journey is how and where I will transform you into my likeness.

# The Bible on the Yellow Line

When God decides He is going give you the desires
of your heart, get ready! You just might be launched into
a world of wonderment.

Early in our married years, there was a man at church selling the Bible on cassette tape. The cost was twenty dollars. Then, twenty dollars might as well have been one thousand dollars. Have you ever just really desired something that was simply way out of your means? Well, you get the picture.

We decided to start collecting our change. We saved for several months. Finally, the week came when we were going to be able to purchase the Bible on cassette. Nathan took the jar of change to the bank and exchanged it for a nice, crisp, twenty dollar bill.

Sunday came, and while getting ready for church, Nathan sensed the Lord was telling him to give our twenty dollars to a particular man we knew and tell him to take his wife out to dinner. After a bit of arguing with the Lord—after Nathan told the Lord, "I never get to take my wife out for dinner, so why should we give this money to someone else so he can take his wife out?"—he relented.

Nathan finally conceded and did as he felt directed.

At a break in the service Sunday morning, Nathan told the man who was selling the tapes that we wouldn't be able to buy those tapes after all. Then he went over to the other man and did as the Lord had instructed him. Then with tears in his eyes, the man told Nathan, "Today is our wedding anniversary, and just this morning I asked the Lord to provide money so I could take my wife out to dinner."

Needless to say, Nathan instantly felt better about the loss of the tapes!

As Paul Harvey would say, "And now . . . the *rest* of the story."

Earlier that morning my mom had called and invited us over for Sunday dinner after church. So we went a different way home from church that day because of heading to my parents. As we headed down Route 42, we noticed something lying in the middle of the road. We slowed down and stopped. Nathan opened his door and looked down in utter astonishment as he picked up a brand new set of the Bible on cassette tape.

It was even the same version we were going to purchase!

There was one tape missing though, but hey, wow, that was okay. We snatched it up and began to head down the road again. Just seconds down the road, though, lo and behold, the missing tape was on the right side of the road on the other yellow line. We stopped once again and then went our way with a complete Bible on cassette in our hands.

What great lengths God goes to in order to bless His children! What creativity flows from His throne to simply show forth His glory and acts of kindness upon the earth!

*Delight yourself in the Lord, and he will give you the desires of your heart.* (Psalm 37:4 ESV)

---

# GOD'S WHISPER

Can you tell me where you are standing at this moment? Is it in a spot where my raindrops of glory can reach you? I am asking you to step closer today. I have things for you to find and dreams to give your tired heart. Why do you hold me at arm's length? I will tell you. You equate how man has treated you with me. I tell you it is not a correct equation. You cannot think I act like man and be in the truth. My heart beat is *you*. My passion is to love *you* and help *you* to position yourself to receive it all. There is no limit. There is no expiration date on my affections toward you. Why would I create you to judge and condemn you? I would not. Relax, dear one, and breathe in my loving breath. Be resuscitated and step closer. It's okay. I love you. Let's fly above your circumstances. Let's enjoy one another's company. Could you picture yourself laughing with me? Please do! Open your heart and get ready to receive the many surprise packages I have wrapped up for you.

# Mr. Morrison's Garden

*Sometimes our spiritual vision is impaired. Vision is critical both in the natural and spiritual realms. How you see yourself and what is happening to you is essential.*

---

After our first child was born, I quit my job to be home with our daughter, and we moved out of our one-bedroom apartment into a duplex. At that point in time we didn't even have a car. Nathan worked at the town's hardware store just a block or two away from home, so he was able to walk to work. He was putting in fifty-four hours a week and bringing home about one hundred and fifty dollars per week.

Fortunately, we paid no rent because we made an arrangement with the owner to fix up our side of the duplex in exchange for rent. And a good friend of ours purchased a big car and took us everywhere we needed to go—to church, grocery shopping, and even on a trip to Pennsylvania to visit Nathan's parents. So thankfully, we were getting by.

But one day when Nathan walked home for lunch, our cupboards were bare, and I had prepared two hot dogs to split between the three of us. Suddenly, Nathan slammed his fist on the table in anger and exclaimed, "I work fifty-four hours a week, and there isn't even enough money to buy food!"

It was a come-to-Jesus moment in the Christopher household for sure.

Just then—literally minutes after Nathan's outburst—there was a knock at the door. I went to the door, and there was a lady standing there asking if I was Christy Barr.

I said, "Yes, but that is my maiden name."

She told me she was the daughter of Mr. Morrison. Mr. Morrison was a man who came into the pharmacy where I had worked. He came in every day to buy a newspaper and a candy bar, so I had become very acquainted with him. He was a grandfatherly type, and I enjoyed talking to him very much.

Mr. Morrison's daughter had gone to the pharmacy and found out I was no longer working there as well as where I was living. She told me her father had a very good garden that year and wondered he if he could share some of the excess with us. Of course we said, "Yes!"

Nathan offered to help her carry it, but she said she could get everything.

Words aren't really adequate to explain what happened next. She proceeded to bring in bags, and bags, and bags of groceries—canned goods, frozen foods, refrigerated foods, a large turkey, and just all kinds of groceries.

Interestingly, there was not one item from Mr. Morrison's garden. When she left, I remember just standing there, overwhelmed and speechless. It was a holy moment in our household—one we will never forget. Today Nathan says, "God never underwhelms us, He always overwhelms us with His goodness."

How did Mr. Morrison know? We don't know, but through Mr. Morrison's daughter, God chased us down and supplied our need. He supplied our need plus an overflow. Even the timing was so perfect! We were at the bottom. In the midst of our anger and frustration, God chased us down with His provision.

Once again, we were front-row spectators to the miraculous hand of God taking care of *His kids*. Our foundation of faith was being built stone by stone.

*Give, and it will be given to you. Good measure, pressed down, shaken together, running over, will be put into your lap.*

(Luke 6:38a ESV)

## GOD'S WHISPER

Abundance. That word started with me. I am very aware of what you have need of. Anxiety is knocking at your door. Will you let him in? Fear wants to penetrate your heart. What will you say to fear? Perseverance is critical to the formation of your soul. Impatience will tear your soul apart. Impatience is the mother of anger. When you take your trust and offer it to your emotions, you will sink in the quicksand of your choice. The game changer will be when you can enjoy peace in the face of unchanging circumstances. The pivotal point will unfold when you choose joy instead of bitterness. The one who pleases me walks in faith in the face of pain and shifting sand. Arise, my child. Take my hand, and I will pull you up and give you a seat beside me. I will possess you with sight, and you will have the upper hand as you step into the glory realm. Glory-vision will cause you to ascend into the heavens and not be moved by earthly trauma. For the sorrows of this world are a vapor in the light of all eternity. So in your plight, remember I have a plan. Look to me, dear one, and I will help you. Abundant living belongs to every one of my children. This means living above and not below, or in spite of your circumstances. Abundance starts with you thinking *my* thoughts.

# Fire Escape

A heart moved by the still, small voice of God can create an
impact on this earth felt for many generations to follow.

One cold Ohio winter, Nathan had to make a run to the junkyard
for a part. Our four-year-old daughter, Bethany, asked her daddy
if she could ride along. So daddy and daughter got in the car and
headed to the junkyard.

Along the way the sleepy girl dozed off, and by the time they
arrived at the junkyard, Nathan saw that Bethany was enjoying
a nice rest and decided to just let her stay in the locked, warm
car. He walked up the hill, with the car in plain sight, to retrieve
the part he needed. As he began the trek up the hill, he heard the
Lord tell him to go back, get Bethany, and bring her with him.

After a moment of deliberation, he decided to turn around,
go back to the car, and get her. After the job was finished they
headed back down the hill to the car. On their way, they were met
by a man running toward them and yelling to Nathan to tell him
his car was on fire!

The man was frantic because he had previously seen a child in there. The car was locked and filled with smoke. Nathan hurried to the car, unlocked and opened the door, and then the smoke-filled car burst into flames. When all was settled, it was discovered that a short in the driver's power seat had started the fire.

I asked my daughter what she remembered about that occurrence since she was so young. She said she remembers falling asleep on the way to the junkyard, and she remembers seeing the hole where the fire burned through the seat where her head once had lain.

When one is tuned in to listening and paying attention to God's voice, there are opportunities for us to be saved and protected from a myriad of dangers and trouble. Just as human sight and hearing are beneficial in the natural realm, spiritual sight and hearing catapult us into places of safety and protection.

If you are a Christian, never ignore the still small voice that comes to you. Rather, embrace it, act upon it, and become a student of God's voice. He does speak to all who will listen.

Imagine that. The eternal God of the universe has something to say to me! He wants to give *me* a heads-up and upper hand in life. He is all about walking with me just as He did with Adam. He wants to enjoy fellowship with His children just like He did with Adam and Eve in the Garden of Eden.

That's what the cross of Jesus Christ opened up for us. It opened up the blockage between me and my Father in Heaven.

*Whether you turn to the right or to the left, your ears will hear a voice behind you, saying, "This is the way; walk in it."*
(Isaiah 30:21)

*My sheep hear my voice, and I know them, and they follow me.*
(John 10:27 KJV)

## GOD'S WHISPER

When you bend your ear to my voice, you will be amazed at what you might hear. One who steps out of the boat of status-quo enters into a realm where it's possible to dance to the musical atmosphere of heaven. I will tell you secrets. I will give you clues and keys to find places no one else has found yet. There is a pioneering spirit in my heart. There is a land we have to reach. The battles will be fierce and even dangerous, yet traveling together will mean safety not found when traveling alone. There are stones to uncover and flowering fields to run through. I have kingdoms for you to conquer and banquet tables to feast upon. I have plans to shame the adversary and raise you up for mighty triumphs. It will be anything but boring. Mostly it will be one of the most beautiful friendships you have ever had. Me and you, and you and me—how about it?

# 5

# Disappearing Rock

To wear the lens of faith means to be able to see what God says in His Word, and His intentions for me have more authority than my current emotional state or trial.

Did you ever have a really nasty day of difficult circumstances? Yes, I'm sure you have. I was having one of those. It was a North Carolina spring day, and we were in the process of building a new house. I was surrounded by circumstantial frustration, sickness, and sadness.

My whole family was sick with the flu all week. My children were missing days at school, and my husband was home from work trying to recover. Then that morning I received a phone call telling me my grandmother in Ohio had just died.

The new house we were building was across the street from where we lived. That day, Johnny, our septic man, was trying to install two septic tanks six feet deep and thirteen feet square.

There was only one approved location where the tanks could sit. But everywhere he put the bucket of his backhoe down to dig, he hit rock six inches down.

It was a day of utter and complete exasperation.

I decided to walk across the street where we were building and just talk to the Lord. I began meditating on Bible stories—like the parting of the Red Sea for instance. I started singing that familiar song, *God Will Make a Way* ("God will make a way where there seems to be no way").[7]

I just remember trusting God for the impossible situation Johnny was dealing with. I didn't know how, but I knew the Lord would work on our behalf. Somehow, those septic tanks were going to find a place in our new yard.

Johnny told us he was up until 2:00 am that night pacing the floor about the job. He told us something just told him to return the next day and try again. He showed up at 6:30 am with his equipment. As he tried one more time, in went the bucket until a hole was dug six feet down for both tanks!

At six feet down, he came to rock once again. It wasn't just rock, though. It was *flat* rock! And because of that, there wasn't even a need to level the tanks. It's mind boggling, really.

Even thinking about that again now simply amazes me. God will make a way where there seems to be no way.[8] There is no place for hopelessness in the life of a child of God. When you are facing a *mountain*, how you process the difficulty, pain, or challenge will greatly determine your personal growth.

---

7  *God Will Make a Way*, by Don Moen, Integrity's Hosanna! Music, 1990.
8  "This is what the Lord says—he who made a way through the sea, a path through the mighty waters, who drew out the chariots and horses, the army and reinforcements together, and they lay there, never to rise again, extinguished, snuffed out like a wick: 'Forget the former things; do not dwell on the past. See, I am doing a new thing! Now it springs up; do you not perceive it? I am making a way in the wilderness and streams in the wasteland'" (Isaiah 43:16-19.

I believe God allows adversity for our personal growth. Walking toward adversity in the power of the Holy Spirit will propel you into places of deeper intimacy with God. And choosing to arm yourself with the power available to you will bring you into places where you will enjoy the presence, the joy, and the peace of God no matter what is happening around you. Succumbing to perplexity and hardship with a victim mentality will not bear the fruit in your life God intends you to bear.

Whether God changes your circumstances or not, you need to win the battle in your mind. Remember the passage in Job chapter thirteen where Job declared, *"Though he slay me, yet will I trust him."* [9]

Winning the battle in our minds is not about our circumstances changing. It's about what lens I am using as I walk through my times of trouble and adversity. Job basically lost everything except for his trust in God. Using the lens of faith and hope is underrated. In fact, faith is the number one attribute to possess for the one God smiles upon.

Henry Ford said, "When everything seems to be going against you, remember the airplane takes off against the wind, not with it."[10]

When the winds are blowing against you, that's your moment to lift off the runway of this old earth and fly with the Holy Spirit to the dimensions of grace and glory that you were wired for. You were wired to fly, rule, and enjoy the heavenly realms where Jesus is seated now. You were created for the very purpose of co-laboring with God in the earth.

I heard Beth Moore speak, and she said, "Throw your shoulders back, pull out your sword, and slice the wind, because it is time to fight like you mean it!"

We must attach our faith to what is true, even when the relentless lies of hell are nipping at our heels. Satan loves to get

---

9   Job 13:15 NKJV.
10  https://www.brainyquote.com/quotes/henry_ford_132651

us to doubt what God said. He thrives on turning our heads and getting us to focus our attention elsewhere. If he can distract our gaze from the One who has created us to carry truth, then we will become spiritually handicapped and paralyzed—and therefore hindered from proceeding forward into our destiny.

We always have choices to make, and sometimes we are our own worst enemy.

What if I hadn't walked across the street and prayed? What if I hadn't employed my faith?

In a short time span, my grandmother went to heaven; my family got well; and the rock disappeared.

*The rocks are broken into pieces by Him.* (Nahum 1:6b ESV)

*However, when the Son of Man comes, will he find faith on the earth?* (Luke 18:8b)

---

## GOD'S WHISPER

There is nothing too difficult with me—nothing. What mountain are you facing this moment? Come to me. Tell me what is going on. Entrust your situation to the One who sees and knows all. I have a ways-and-means committee that is out of this world! As you evaluate your trial, be sure to calculate with me in mind. For I am the X factor in your equation. It will all make sense as you look back on what you now face. Worry, fear, and dread wish to crown your head and create jeers and taunts straight from the pit of darkness. I have called you to rule. I have called you to declare what is okay and what is not okay as you walk in fellowship with my Holy Spirit. It's okay to say, "This mountain will move!" It's not acceptable to my heart to see you roll over and simply take everything the adversary pitches at you. I have given you authority over all of his deeds of darkness. I allow him to touch you at times so you may gain strength and choose stability in the Spirit over cowering in fear and discouragement. But come on now! Get up and go to the place that intimidates you the most and begin speaking—causing it to line up with heaven. For I will not do what I have told *you* to do, yet remember you cannot do what *I* only can do.

# 6

# Paid In Full

To get a full grip on what heaven is doing with your current dilemma is to grab destiny by the tail and call it your own!

---

We had five bills totaling thirty-five thousand dollars. One day as Nathan was praying for the Lord to help us, he saw (in his mind's eye) the Lord go to the drawer where we kept our bills. The Lord took the five bills out of the drawer, wrapped a red ribbon around them, then took a stamp and stamped it "Canceled."

Nathan said to the Lord, "Just as you have shown me, go ahead and do it."

That year was a year of loss where Nathan worked. He was paid his normal salary, but he had recently been told there would be no year-end profit sharing as in previous years.

A few days later, Nathan went into the company office to pick up the latest paperwork for the homes they were building at that time. He got back in the truck and put all the retrieved paperwork on the front seat. As he drove down the road, he noticed that an envelope with his name on it fell to the floor from the pile. At his next stop he opened up the envelope to find a check for twenty-five thousand dollars.

He called his boss and questioned him about the check. His boss told him that even though there were major losses, he knew Nathan had worked very hard that year and wanted to at least give him that. He knew nothing of our financial crunch.

We took the money, paid tithe on it, and then proceeded to pay off four of the five debts that Nathan saw the Lord mark "Canceled."

A couple of months passed, and one last debt was still hanging around. Nathan prayed again and said, "Lord, you so quickly took care of the first four bills, go ahead and take care of the last one!"

We owed $13,500 to a friend who offered to loan us the money to purchase land to build our house on. He wasn't pressing us for it, but we really needed to be released of debt. A few days later, though, we received an envelope from that friend.

Nathan immediately thought he would be requesting his money. That man was going through a divorce and took a major financial loss because of it. In the envelope was a small receipt (like the ones a waitress writes on at a restaurant). At the top of the receipt was written "Nathan Christopher." In the middle was written, "$13,500." And at the bottom, it was stamped with a rubber stamp, "CANCELED."

It was just as Nathan had seen it when he was praying. Nathan called our friend to see what was up. He said he had his divorce settlement a week earlier. When he left the courthouse he sat on the steps and prayed, "Lord, how will I ever pull out of this loss?"

He then said the Lord spoke to him and said, "If you want to recover from the payout for the divorce, you can start by canceling the debt to Nathan Christopher."

He said he struggled with it for a few days, but knew he had to do it! He told us later that within six months he had received back all of the money he had to pay out for his divorce and more. He also told us it probably wouldn't have happened if he hadn't canceled our debt.

Oh the matchless love and care of our God!

It was in communion with God when Nathan received a vision of what God wanted to do. As we cast our burdens upon Him, He sees, and He already knows what He wants to do. At times, receiving miracles requires our spiritual vision and focus. We must not be moved by what we see to the point where we become hopeless. Rather, as we see our predicament, our eyes must turn heavenward for the *God-solutions* we so need!

The creativity of God overwhelms me. He orchestrates such detail at times when He comes to our rescue. We are constantly learning that for every situation troubling us, there is a more-than-equal place in the Spirit in which to live and prosper.

*Consider it pure joy, my brothers and sisters, whenever you face trials of many kinds, because you know that the testing of your faith produces perseverance. Let perseverance finish its work so that you may be mature and complete, not lacking anything.* (James 1:2-4)

*Now unto him that is able to do exceeding abundantly above all that we ask or think, according to the power that worketh in us . . .* (Ephesians 3:20 KJV)

## GOD'S WHISPER

Beloved, heaven is backing you up. Angels are standing at attention listening for my orders to minister to you. A great cloud of witnesses is surrounding you, cheering you onward and upward! You are surrounded by my songs of deliverance. Your heart is beautiful, and your personality is just as I intended; for you reflect a part of me no one else can. For each adversity, I have something for you to do. Your first job is to simply trust me because you love me, and I love you. Is there ever any other reason to trust someone? Out of that love-union will come words and emotions and directives that will help you along the way as you trek through the hot sands of the journey. There will be regular tests that will produce a glorious testimony of my goodness as you suffer long with me through the predicament and perplexities of this world. Take heart now, my beloved. You will finish fine—and with a victor's crown as you persevere and follow my instructions along the way. Our trust will be the mortar between the bricks of the glorious structure I am building in you.

# 7

# Game Boy Color

God invented the word *surprise*.

Our son Levi was about ten years old, and his birthday was approaching. That year, a new game was released called *Game Boy Color*. It was a pricey gadget. Our son, Levi, expressed his deep desire to have one, and it was one of those times as a parent when you want to run to the store and get just what your child wants.

Extravagance is fun for a parent when it comes to giving things to our children. Don't we just love giving our children what they desire? (It's an echo of the Father's heart for us.) Levi's heart was to have one of those games, and our heart was to get it for him. The problem was—you guessed it—no money.

As was their custom, one day Levi went to work with Nathan to earn a few extra dollars. They were traveling down the road when they noticed something on the berm beside the road. They stopped to investigate, and to their amazement, they had found a Game Boy Color in nearly perfect condition. But even more amazing, already in it was the exact game Levi wanted.

Wow! That was a wordless wonder performed at the hands of our loving Father.

Why do we put God in a box? Why do we think He needs to perform according to our limited understanding? I challenge you today to ask Him to expand your thinking. I dare you to take the lid off of your human-sized God. Our God is a roaring, untamed lion. He is to be feared, revered, and loved for the incredible, beyond-our-imagination God He is.

Take a deep breath right now. Breathe in—by faith—new truths you haven't yet learned. Say to the Holy Spirit, "You have permission to expand my thoughts. You have the green light to blow me away with your acts of kindness. I want to know you in ways I could never imagine. Reveal yourself to me and surprise me according to *your* intentions for me. I receive this new wave of knowing you in Jesus name. Amen."

*Behold, these are but the outskirts of his ways, and how small a whisper do we hear of him! But the thunder of his power who can understand?* (Job 26:14 ESV)

*No one's ever seen or heard anything like this, never so much as imagined anything quite like it—what God has arranged for those who love him.*

*But you've seen and heard it because God by his Spirit has brought it all out into the open before you.*
(1 Corinthians 2:9-10 MSG)

## GOD'S WHISPER

What can't I do? I say again, am I limited in how I bless you? Do you have a human-fashioned perimeter box in your heart where you think I should hang out? May I have permission to overrun your logic from time to time and show you another dimension of life with me? The truth is, your mind wasn't built to contain all my glorious acts and deeds. If you operate out of your intellect, you will limit me in your life by the pure logic of your mind. When you walk in step with my Holy Spirit, all will be possible, and there will be automatic trust in the creativity of my ways with you. Step over the threshold of reason. Often, my tools and devices of working will offend your mind. As a matter of fact, look at how often I offended the mind of the spiritual leaders of the day when I walked the earth in the flesh. I offended them to the degree they killed me. I say to you, kill your intellect when it comes to walking in the Spirit, or your intellect will deaden you to what I am doing. You need your mind to think and operate in this world, but if you only use your mind when it comes to loving me, you will miss out on the amazing horizons and scenery of what I want to show you as you pioneer forward.

# 8

# Go For It

Simple child-like faith dissolves the dark weapons that have
been formed against us.

I started writing this book just three days ago. I have been quite
absorbed in the works of God in our lives. It has been shaking
me to the core to meditate on the miraculous hand of God. You
see, events similar to those in these stories of many years ago yet
continue to happen on a regular basis.

The supernatural is our normal.

Nathan is one of the most hard-working men I have ever
known. He's not afraid to get dirty and do what it takes to make
a living. He is a carpenter by trade—and a very excellent one at
that. Yesterday was a difficult day at work physically, and he came
home in much back pain from all the lifting. As we prayed before
we went to bed, I had a strong impression to just lay hands on his
back and pray for healing.

God says in His Word, when we lay our hands on the sick
they will recover.[11] I'm still learning what this means, and there

11  Mark 16:17-18.

have been times after prayer that the person I prayed over didn't recover but even died. While writing this book on miracles, signs, and wonders, I had a very good friend die from a three-year-long, grueling battle with cancer. I prayed and fasted and believed, but God took her to heaven.

I admit that threw me. I was sad and disappointed—and even upset at the Lord. I didn't understand why she wasn't healed. Yet experiences like that are not going to deter me from praying! I am going to remain faithful to what God asked me to do in His Word and leave the results up to Him. God always knows what is best, and His wisdom surpasses all other.

So I told Nathan to stand up. I wanted to lay my hands on his back and pray. You see, I had a picture in my head of us standing and me putting my hand on his back, speaking to the pain, and telling it to leave my husband's body. So I acted on the picture that came to my mind. I believe it was a picture from the Holy Spirit instructing me what to do.

We stood up, and I began to pray with my hand on the place of his pain. As believers we have authority from God to pray and overcome all the power of the enemy.[12] We have authority over all the works of darkness. I feel like I am in elementary school— and there is so much to learn—but I am learning and discovering more and more how faith and spiritual authority works.

I spoke to the pain and inflammation and called his back into alignment. I prayed several times and then asked Nathan each time if the pain was any different. Each time, he said the pain was less. I prayed until he told me the pain was gone. Nathan then told me about the pain and stiffness in his hands and fingers. So we did the same thing for those problems. Praise be to God, my husband went to bed pain free!

12 "I have given you authority to trample on snakes and scorpions and to overcome all the power of the enemy; nothing will harm you" (Luke 10:19).

There are times in our day-to-day lives with God when we need to step out of our boats of comfort and follow His call into the waters of faith and obedience. Well, I was stepping out of my boat that night in confronting my husband's pain.

We may look foolish for a moment as we exhibit our faith, but so did Noah until the first drop of rain kissed the earth where the freshly completed ark stood.

One Sunday morning I heard our pastor say these words: "I would rather be a wet-water walker than a dry-boat sitter."

Folks, this is real. I'm telling you, the power of Jesus Christ is available for all who are sick and troubled. Reader, just think about it. Expand your view of God. Let Him take you to places you've never been! Do things you've never done. Get out of the boat and start walking on your water. Jesus is out there with hand extended to you, saying, "Come."[13]

> *And these signs will follow those who believe: In My name they will cast out demons; they will speak with new tongues; they will take up serpents; and if they drink anything deadly, it will by no means hurt them; they will lay hands on the sick, and they will recover.* (Mark 16:17-18 NKJV)

## GOD'S WHISPER

Step out of the boat of comfort. Put your foot into the footprint of Jesus. Journey toward the "greater things you will do" that Jesus spoke of.[14] Engage your faith. Try

---

13 "Lord, if it's you," Peter replied, "tell me to come to you on the water." "Come," he said. Then Peter got down out of the boat, walked on the water and came toward Jesus" (Mathew 14:28-29).

14 "Very truly I tell you, whoever believes in me will do the works I have been doing, and they will do even greater things than these, because I am going to the Father" (John 14:12).

it. You are growing in the knowledge of my intent for the world. My love swirls all around you wondering if you will absorb yet another ounce of it and be influenced by it. For as you are influenced and constrained by my love, I can launch you into your loveless world to create impact. I didn't create you for failure. I didn't form you for mediocrity. Nor did I build you for complacency. I brought you into existence so we would spread my glory and fame all over the earth. I wanted to share with you. I could have done it all without you. But I didn't. Spread your *spirit and truth* wings and jump. Step off the cliff of the familiar into the atmosphere of heaven. It's all around you!

# 9

# Fragrance of Heaven

A sign or wonder from heaven is merely God's expression of His
creative intentions to cause us to turn our head and remember
His loving presence with us.

In Acts 2:43, Luke mentioned the many signs and wonders that
were being performed by the apostles. Many signs and wonders
were occurring in the days of the early Church.

The Greek word for *signs* is the word *sēmeion*.[15] It speaks of an
unusual occurrence, transcending the common course of nature.

The Greek word for *wonders* is the word *teras*. It refers to
something so strange as to cause it to be watched or observed.
It relays that emotion excited by novelty, or the presentation
to the sight or mind of something new, unusual, strange, great,

---

15  Unless otherwise noted, all Hebrew and Greek definitions were derived
   from https://eliyah.com/lexicon.html.

extraordinary, or not well understood; surprise; astonishment; admiration; amazement.

Now I have a story to tell.

It was a normal Saturday afternoon. I decided to go with my husband to visit and pray for a friend of ours, who was in the hospital fighting for his life in a battle with cancer. We got into the car and headed down the road. After just a couple of minutes I looked at my husband only to see him looking at me. I asked him if he smelled something. He said, "Yes."

Was it on our clothes? Was it coming through the vents? The moment was pregnant with mystery and wonder.

Where was that burning, sweet fragrance coming from?

It smelled like incense. It suddenly filled the car. Its aroma strengthened, and my husband's eyes began to burn. As we drove along Lohr Road we suddenly pinpointed the source.

My right hand.

Not my left hand, just my right hand. There was only one thing to do. I put my hand to my face to simply inhale that heavenly fragrance. I simply couldn't stop smelling the unusual aroma! And then, almost as quickly as we identified the fragrance on my right hand, my husband said his right hand, as well, had that sweet-smelling aroma.

We drove along for forty amazing minutes until we reached the hospital. We went into our friend's room and shared our experience with him. Our hands still carried the aroma as we visited and prayed with him. The room filled with such otherworldly peace and assurance—causing us to sit in simple amazement and wonder.

It was a moment indeed—a holy moment for sure.

As we prayed, we held our hands close so our friend could also share in the joy of the heavenly fragrance. The fragrance was slightly different on each of our hands. At one point, our friend took my husband's right hand and just held it close to his face. I watched in utter amazement as he breathed in the fragrance like he was smelling a flower in heaven. Time seemed suspended for a moment that Saturday afternoon.

It was time to go. We left the hospital and enjoyed the same *aura* of heaven the whole way home. Shortly after we got in our house, it left. It left just as suddenly as it came. We had been sideswiped by the glory of God—suddenly, undoubtedly, and swiftly.

Could God have just wanted to accompany us in such a way that there could be no doubt of His attendance in our Saturday afternoon prayer meeting? The questions arise, yet in my spirit I know I am to just savor the moment and smile at God, who takes pleasure in breezing in upon His children and bringing special gifts of joy and comfort.

It was wonderful. It was captivating. The mystery of it will always nestle in my heart.

Do we always need an explanation of God's actions? I think not. Some things are meant just to be savored and enjoyed. Our friend crossed over to his heavenly destination a few weeks later. There was no healing for him on this side of heaven, but I wonder to this day if God was just saying it was his time and gave all three of us a foretaste of the heavenly glory he was soon to enjoy.

*Everyone was filled with awe at the many wonders and signs performed by the apostles.* (Acts 2:43)

## GOD'S WHISPER

The mountain peaks and the valley depths cannot begin to measure the expanse of how I think and the ways I want to engage with mankind. It's my desire and wish to invade your earth-tethered thinking on a regular basis. I put you into this earth to display my glory-realm that is as near as your breath. What does it really mean to be filled with my Holy Spirit? I can hardly wait to explain it! You are to confront with my kindness. You are to lead with my love. You are to talk the language of truth. You are to flow like the wind at my beck and call. As you are in this world, act like a foreigner, because you are. As you study my word, I can teach you to think my thoughts. As you think my thoughts and love with my love, your ambassadorship will be perfected, and the aroma of heaven will always be swirling about you. Jesus was different when He walked upon the earth. They didn't know what to do with Him. Some were offended. Some were intrigued. Others followed, and one betrayed. Many became disciples, and others thought murderous thoughts. Your life should create all types of reactions as you walk with me. As we walk together and I touch you, minds will be offended, but have hope. Those who truly seek me will be attracted to the peculiar life you have. It's never about pleasing man. It's always about pleasing me. For in that place of union with me lies your protection and all the things you will ever need on this earth and beyond.

# 10

# The Arms of God

There are moments when we are chilled to the bone in fear, when God simply opens His arms and invites us in for the embrace of all embraces. In that moment of perfect love, all fear is truly driven out.

---

I am in a continual state of discovering just how deep the love of God is for me. This one thing carries me through every danger, toil, and snare.

It was a cool fall Ohio day. I remember it well. It was one of those "I remember exactly where I was when I got the word" sort of moments. I had just pulled in to work. I was working part time as Direct Care Staff for adults with developmental disabilities.

A couple of days prior to that day, Nathan had lifted something heavy at work. That caused a strain in the same eye that had the detached retina years earlier. His vision began to be strange. He knew time was of the essence, so he went to the eye specialist. I needed to go to work that day, so when I received the call from him, and he told me he was to go into emergency surgery the following day, my heart hit the floor.

Nathan was our primary breadwinner, I was just working to help out. Following surgery he was to remain face down for about ten weeks except for bathroom and showering breaks. That meant basically no income for this paycheck-to-paycheck family. We had just built a large house, and our mortgage payments were pretty sizable.

The surgery went well, and he commenced upon the road to recovery. Sunday was a couple of days after surgery. I went to church by myself in need of a fresh touch from heaven. In my spirit I knew God would take care of us, but in my soul I was scared, rattled, and simply undone. At the end of the service, a very tall man (a surgeon friend of ours) came to me and put his arms out to hug me.

As I fell into his embrace I felt as if the literal arms of my *Papa-God* were wrapping around me over and over again in an unending hug. Fears, worries, and anxieties literally drained out of me to the floor. Our friend's name was Dan. He said to me, "If you need anything, anything at all, I want you to call me. I'm very serious."

Even though it was Dan's voice that I heard, I knew in the core of my being that I had come into direct contact with my Father in heaven. It was so real. I can hear him say now just like it was this morning, "If you need anything, anything at all, I want you to call me. I'm very serious."

Friend, I sense that Papa-God is speaking the same to you. If you are in need at this moment, call to Him. He is so serious about you turning to Him in your time of need!

Over the course of the next three to four months, every bill was paid. We had all we needed. Someone came up to us and wanted to pay our electric bills for three months. Someone else came up to us and wanted to make our house payments for three months. We received gift cards and checks in the mail. Getting the mail became a moment of humbling gratefulness as we received support literally from all over the country from friends and family who were gathering around us in our time of need.

All in all, we received gifts of over eleven thousand dollars by the end of that season. We never missed a beat financially or got behind on anything while I worked part time and my husband was face down in recovery mode.

It was incredible.

Sometimes I am slow to catch on, and I forget to put on the lens of faith. My Father is so patient in teaching me though. He is gentle toward me. He understands my frailty, and He continually calls me under His wing of greatness.

God pulls me in and situates me in His *love-covering*. As I nestle down into the blankets of divine love, the comfort and courage that floods my gloomy soul dispels the darkness and calms my fears. I am instantly catapulted into His loving lap to enjoy the ride of His provision and protection.

Recently I told my husband that when he tells me we have a surprise four hundred and fifty dollar furnace repair bill (which just happened the other day), I want my first thought not to be of fear. I fear, then I move into trust. Why couldn't I train myself to trust first?

Hmm, maybe one day that will be my story. I do believe I'm getting closer.

> *"Don't be afraid," the prophet answered. "Those who are with us are more than those who are with them."* (2 Kings 6:16)

## GOD'S WHISPER

Knowing me gives you the upper hand. Knowing about me only keeps you locked up in your circumstantial cell of fear and worry. Knowing me, and having conversations with me, means there is a relationship. At times I come to your rescue in order to bring the reality check you need to stand in the place of faith and not fear. I know you are trying. I understand your frailty. At other times I act as a teacher would when giving a test to his students. I say nothing, and I keep quiet because the student needs to recall what I have already taught and apply it. You see, each moment is a gift, whether it is a time of ease or a time of conflict. The ebb and flow of life is exactly what you need to grow and flourish in my house. Don't fear the storm. Rather, lean into me for covering, safety, and directions. Each challenge contains gems for you. Every time you are catapulted into a new fiery furnace, the treasure hunt begins. There are things found in the furnace you will not find elsewhere. Each gem makes you rich as you embrace the trouble in the power of my Holy Spirit. In the refiner's fire, you will be purified. The pure in heart get to see me. The pure in heart grow in not only the knowledge of me but also the knowing of me. I want to walk with you. I want you to walk with me. You are clean. You are in right standing with me. It's all paid for. You can't do any more or less for my approval. You are approved—end of discussion. Now let's get on with it. There is a Kingdom to build. There are exploits to perform, and there is an eternity to enjoy with me.

# 11

# Miracle Under the Gas Tank Lid

At times, miracles, signs, and wonders are as close
as our next breath.

At the time, we were at the point once again where every penny
literally mattered. Nathan needed to put gas in his truck. The only
option of payment was to gather up all the coins in the console
of his truck and see how much gas he was really going to be able
to get.

Embarrassed, he gathered about a dollar and a half in assorted
coins and took them to the cashier. The cashier jeered and asked
Nathan if he really wanted to put *all* of it in gas. Humiliated,
Nathan went to the pump to begin pumping.

What happened next simply messes with my brain to this day.

He opened the lid to access the gas cap, and to his wonderment, there—just sitting on top of the cap—were two, folded, ten-dollar bills. Standing there in a frozen moment of surprise, he removed the bills and pumped his pre-paid gas. Too put out at the attendant to take the miracle money in and get more gas, he went home and shared his story with me. We each had ten dollars to put fuel in our vehicles for work the next day.

How does God think of this stuff?

Yes, I know He's God and can do anything. I hope there are special movie theaters in heaven where we can view the rest of our stories—like angels putting things in places where we found them, or when our angels had to work double time on our behalf to turn a potential disastrous accident into a near miss.

I am in a continual state of awe.

*Rain in abundance, O God, you shed abroad; you restored your inheritance as it languished; Your flock found a dwelling in it; in your goodness, O God, you provided for the needy.*
(Psalm 68:9-10 ESV)

---

## GOD'S WHISPER

Child, what concerns you today? Surrender it. What storms are tossing your soul in this moment? Tell your soul to be still, and remind it that I am God. Is there emotional pain of betrayal or grief? Come to me, and I will bring comforting strength. Listen to the voice of love. Listen to the voice of destiny. This is merely a stepping-stone season for you and me to gather strength together and regroup. You will emerge ready. You will come out of this place with your sword sharpened and your shield shining! Your sphere of influence is about to expand as you keep pace with me now. I am sheltering you, and as my shadow covers you, there is a sweet download of pure glory and joy entering your vessel. I am going to empower and train you to respond only to my love and intentions for you. Unhealthy trigger points of fear and frustration are coming off of you in this valley of uncertainty and pain. My love is encapsulating you as you continue to reach out of the natural and into the eternal realm of possibilities. As you pursue the open doors I am giving you, you will be greeted with favor and opportunities meant only for you.

# 12

# Gracious Father

*Just as we enjoy surprising our children with random goodness and gifts, we likewise have a Heavenly Father who has moments in His heart when He simply wants to do stuff for us! He can't help it. He is simply good.*

We had decided to move back to Ohio after a nine year season of living in North Carolina. We also decided to build a house. When you live with a carpenter, building a new home is always an attractive option when it comes to where you will live. And it just so happened that some property came up for sale just around the corner from my parents' farm.

We were then delighted when a friend of ours approached us and offered to loan us $36,000 to purchase the property in exchange for a business proposition on how we could pay him back. It seemed like the right thing for us to do, and it seemed to be a door God was opening for us. So with the $36,000 in hand, we purchased the land and began to build our new home.

Shortly after construction began, though, our friend changed his mind and decided the business agreement wasn't going to work for him. But we still needed to pay him back. Not too long after that, the market crashed, and work for a carpenter became difficult to find. The man then began to pressure us for his money.

That became a heavy burden on our shoulders, and we prayed and cried out to God for help. One day the man called Nathan and wanted him to come into his office. Dreading the meeting, we were sure the man was going to demand instant payment for what we owed him.

What had we gotten ourselves into? The atmosphere felt heavy and depressive. In all of our adventures up until that point one would think we would have been full of faith and trust. But the truth of the matter was, we were trembling in fearful discouragement.

How slow we are to learn at times. I can understand why Jesus said to His disciples on more than one occasion, *"O ye of little faith!"* [16]

Nathan went to meet the man. They went into his office, and what happened next became another story of the glorious acts of God in our lives. Sitting across the desk from the man, he showed Nathan a piece of paper. On the paper was written, "Nathan Christopher," then the amount owed, "$36,000." He asked Nathan if that was the correct amount. Nathan confirmed it was.

The man then proceeded to ask Nathan, "What would you do if I did this?"

---

16 "Wherefore, if God so clothe the grass of the field, which to day is, and to morrow is cast into the oven, shall he not much more clothe you, O ye of little faith?" (Matthew 6:30 KJV).

"And he saith unto them, 'Why are ye fearful, O ye of little faith?' Then he arose, and rebuked the winds and the sea; and there was a great calm" (Matthew 8:26 KJV).

He then took his pen and put an X over the amount and wrote the word, "CANCELED."

Nathan asked him what he was doing. The man simply said, "This."

He then pushed the paper across the desk to Nathan and proceeded to tell him the matter would never come up again.

And it never has.

Oh the matchless wonders of God! Can His works be explained by the human mind? Never! Even in our faithlessness, He still wants to do things for us. He is elated to show His glory and intent for us. At times He asks things of us in return for what He has done for us, and then there are times when He just proves himself to be the gracious Father who goes out and does things for His kids *just because*!

The Lord is always making an imprint upon our hearts. The imprint says, "You are mine, and I will never leave or forsake you."[17]

With each passing test, our faith's muscle-mass strengthens. The next time you are in a place of challenge, put in your mind the times God worked and amazed you. Why would this time be any different? He might not work the same way, but either way, God is up to something, and you can just trust that He is going to care for you in the midst of your valley-view.

Go ahead, lean into His breast. He will cover you. Nestle down into His loving intentions for you. Your adversary wants you to practice being worried. Your heavenly Father wants you to practice abiding in His presence.

> *Come and see what God has done: he is awesome in his deeds*
> *toward the children of man.* (Psalm 66:5 ESV)

---

17 "Keep your lives free from the love of money and be content with what you have, because God has said, "Never will I leave you; never will I forsake you" (Hebrews 13:5).

# GOD'S WHISPER

Child, relax. I am at work. I have angels positioned around you for this time. They are doing their job. As you sail the high waters of the stormy seas and feel your boat tossing back and forth, remember how I slept in the boat when the storm hit?[18] When you entwine your thoughts with mine, you can sleep well in a storm. This is the benefit of knowing me and my heart for you. You know whose you are, and rest is a by-product of that. Rest is a fruit of a healthy relationship with me. Earth-living presents difficulty and hard labor. Spirit-living immerses you in rest and ease. I have done the work, you simply abide in my finished work. My completed work paid for your liberation from fear, worry, panic, and dread. You are rich and wealthy in my shadow. The tormentor cannot touch one who is enjoying fellowship with me. Fear goes to flight when one is fellowshipping with *Love*.[19] That truth, when bearing fruit in the heart, catapults one into realms of unnatural possibilities. The unthinkable—the unimaginable—is the reality of one walking in step with me. What do you get when you mix a loving God, creativity, and a receptive heart? You get the image of Christ being formed and birthed in one who will shine like the stars in the backdrop of the heavens. You get divine and unique invasions into a world that struggles to see beyond itself. I want to take you places. I want to show you my glory. I want to amaze you, dear one. Let's go!

---

18 Mark 4:36-40.
19 1 John 4:8.

# 13

# Twenty Dollar Deposit

*Sometimes the dream world and the natural world collide in a way that forces us to expand our way of thinking.*

The dream world is mysterious. Why do we dream the dreams we dream? Could there be times in our sleep when there is an invasion of heaven? I think so. Read this story.

One night my husband had a dream. In the dream he was in the lobby of a very nice, old hotel. All of a sudden, what appeared to be a homeless man approached him. The man looked every bit to be someone in need. But he came to Nathan and told him he wanted to bless him and give him twenty dollars.

Thinking the man could use the money for himself, Nathan declined the offer. After conversing with the man and refusing his offer a few times, Nathan walked out through the revolving front door onto the sidewalk. Relentless, though, the man followed him and once again explained he wanted to bless Nathan.

Realizing the man simply wasn't going to take *No* for an answer, Nathan accepted the twenty-dollar gift and placed it in his wallet. The man then displayed a partial smile, turned around, and walked away.

And that was the end of the dream.

The next morning was church. After the service, someone asked Nathan for a phone number. He had a business card in his wallet, so He opened his wallet for the business card. But he opened it only to find a twenty-dollar bill in what Nathan was sure had been an empty wallet. He knew for certain he had no cash in his wallet the evening before.

Nathan double-checked with me and asked if I had put money in there. I told him that I never put money *in* his wallet, but I have been known to take money out of it! What in the world? Immediately, the dream from the previous night came flooding into Nathan's mind.

The natural mind simply cannot comprehend these kinds of happenings.

Words about prophecy, dreams, and visions are recorded all over in the Bible. And in the book of Joel, we have record of a prophecy by Joel that foretold how God would pour out His spirit into the world during the last days.

And in chapter two of the book of Acts, we read that it was on the Day of Pentecost—on the occasion of God pouring out the Holy Spirit upon the believers gathered together in Jerusalem following Christ's ascension—when Peter stood before the people and proclaimed that it was on that very day when God was beginning to fulfill Joel's prophecy.

Folks, I believe the last days began at Pentecost.

We are in those "last days" even now. The next great event will be the return of Jesus for His bride and the great consummation of all things! Right now, though, we are preparing the way of the Lord to come. He is engaging with us and bringing daily hope and love into our hearts and souls. Heaven kisses earth, and earth reaches back for the One who is coming.

Why would God visit Nathan in a dream for a simple twenty dollars? I don't know. Perhaps God did it just to let Nathan know He was still aware and in control. So often the God of heaven and earth simply wants to bend over and kiss us on the head. I think it's that simple—yet that profound at the same time.

> *And it shall come to pass afterward, that I will pour out my Spirit on all flesh; your sons and your daughters shall prophesy, your old men shall dream dreams, and your young men shall see visions.* (Joel 2:28 ESV)

> *And in the last days it shall be, God declares, that I will pour out my Spirit on all flesh, and your sons and your daughters shall prophesy, and your young men shall see visions, and your old men shall dream dreams..* (Acts 2:17 ESV)

## GOD'S WHISPER

I desire you. I created you with a need to belong. I choose you. You belong to me, and I love you, yet love creates choice. You get to choose where to cast your affections and desires. Every longing and desire in your heart can be satisfied in me. I touch you with wonder and grace. I interact with you on so many levels. I am awakening you into the ways and means of my holy activity. I am showing you how intimately involved I really am in your daily affairs. I bless you and then stand back and let you enjoy the pleasures I have given you. For every good and perfect gift really does come from me.[20] I lavish gifts upon you daily. As a matter of fact, my gifts can even become so normal to you that you really don't count them as gifts anymore. But I am awakening you to the gifts that keep coming to you—gifts of stability, peace, happiness, joy, sunshine, rain, food, air, love, relationships, family, friendships, and on and on. Not all enjoy the same gifts, yet all have gifts to unwrap—and the choice to see me in them. I also have gifts of dreams and visions. There are times when I simply want to transport you and take you to places not known in the natural realm. Can you hear this? I want to bump your natural logic and put you into the seat of the heavenly realm. Since you are seated with me in heavenly places,[21] wouldn't it make sense that you would have heavenly experiences? You are a spirit who lives in a body and has a soul. It's true. I will relate to you on a spirit-level. I will interact with you spirit to spirit. I gave you natural eyes to see in the natural realm, but did you know you came with spiritual vision as well? Many choose to walk their spiritual life with their natural vision only. This will produce nothing but frustration and confusion every time. Natural vision is for one purpose only: to see the natural world. Spiritual vision is also for one purpose only: to see the spiritual world paralleling with the natural world. You see, many do not use the

---

20 James 1:17.

21 "But God, who is rich in mercy, because of His great love with which He loved us, even when we were dead in trespasses, made us alive together with Christ . . . and made us sit together in the heavenly places in Christ Jesus, that in the ages to come He might show the exceeding riches of His grace in His kindness toward us in Christ Jesus" (Ephesians 2:4-7).

spiritual vision available to them and have me so boxed in by their natural way of thinking and seeing that they decide I am not even real. I will not fit into your natural box. It's like trying to stuff a hot air balloon into a tin can. It won't happen. What *will* happen is frustration and even anger. In your thoughts, put me into the expanse of the heavens, and there you will find me. Put me beyond the limits of your understanding, and there you will have rest. I fit in eternity. I fit in limitlessness. So get out of your natural-vision-only, and add to it divine, spiritual sight. Know my Word, and you will know what it is to see in the Spirit. Become a student of my activity in my Word, and you will soar like the eagles into realms that will be faithful to confound your natural thinking and sight. Don't be afraid, dear one. I am the One who made you for this. I am the One you are looking for. You are the one I want to reach the world through. You were made to belong with me. You are spirit, and I am awakening you in this hour to new realms of walking with me.

# 14

# Dew-Drenched Grass Marvel

Be watchful, lest you miss the next sight God
wants to amaze you with. He is not in a box. He will
at times astound you to the core.

One weekend we traveled to the eastern side of Tennessee for our
nephew's wedding. It was a Saturday morning. Five of us decided
to go on a mountain hike before the afternoon wedding. I was
kicking myself over and over for leaving my camera at home.
We were in the car on our way to our hiking destination when I
declared, "I wish I would have at least stopped at Walmart on the
way to pick up one of their disposable cameras."

We were an hour or more away from anywhere a store could
be found. I love to take pictures of God's creation, and I was
simply beside myself looking at all the beauty with no camera
to capture it! But eventually I resigned myself to the fact that

I would just need to be content with simply enjoying my time without a camera.

We got out of the car and commenced upon one of the Great Smoky Mountain trails. Me being the lollygagging person I was, I trailed behind the other four hikers. About three to four minutes down the path, I looked to the left and saw something lying in the dew-soaked grass. Could it be? There to my utter amazement was a brand new, dry, disposable, Walmart camera.

In complete, perplexing wonderment, I yelled out to the others about my find. "How could each co-hiker walk past this sight?" I thought. "Why was I the only one to discover this confounding object?" I remember feeling instantly favored on the spot. My Father had seen my desire and sent an angel, or someone, to put that camera in plain view for me only!

It was a jaw-dropping juncture-in-time for this Jesus-loving gal. *Papa* loved me. It was just another expression of His crazy, stringless love. It was a *just-because* minute in time from Him.

One reason we exist is for God's pleasure.[22] We know God loves us, yet have we ever entertained the thought that He really *likes* us too? We bring Him pleasure. I believe God actually wants to have fun with us! At times he interacts with us in ways that are playful and fun. When I spotted that camera in the wet, tall grass that day, I felt the laughter of God raining down upon me in that moment.

Picture a father playing with his little child. Why did God make us ticklish? Did you ever wonder about that? Why do certain bones and muscles, when rubbed or poked, make us laugh and giggle? Picture a father out in the back yard with his young child just rolling around on the ground, laughing and laughing with his child. If it happens in the natural realm, why not in the spiritual realm?

---

22 "Thou art worthy, O Lord, to receive glory and honour and power: for thou hast created all things, and for thy pleasure they are and were created" (Revelation 4:11).

Sometimes God just makes me laugh. There are moments like finding a dry camera in a dew-drenched field—just when I need it—that puts laughter in my soul.

Sometimes when Nathan is playing with our grandchildren and tickling them, they will say, "Tickle me again, Pappy." They actually enjoy being tickled and love the interaction with Pappy. Could it be okay to say to your heavenly Father, *Tickle me Daddy?* I think so. There are holy, solemn moments with God, yet there are also moments of glee and joy that are otherworldly.

Gifts of laughter between God and His children connect heaven and earth like no other.

*Every good and perfect gift is from above, coming down from the Father of the heavenly lights, who does not change like shifting shadows.* (James 1:17)

## GOD'S WHISPER

Child, do you not know I am the author of creativity? I enjoy astounding you. Our friendship is my delight. What we can do in the earth together is beyond what you could think. You in me and I in you make a pair that absolutely confounds our adversary. Father and child, hand in hand, hearts linked together, is my idea of fun! Unless you become childlike at heart, you will miss many simple adventures I have planned for you. Fearless trust is what it takes. Fling away your apprehension, my dear one. Cast off what is restraining you from stepping out of your boat. Do some water-walking with me! You will see I am right. You will discover that life, as you know it now, pales in comparison to the next dimension of the Holy Spirit-living I'm calling you into.

# 15

# A Special Ingredient

Miracles of the heart are the best. When a miracle happens in a heart, anything is possible.

There was a season when there were some painful relational struggles in our family. I won't go in to all who were involved or what the issues were. That's not important in my story. It did involve Nathan, though. He was struggling (as we all do at times) with something someone had done. I, too, had the same struggle, but by God's grace I had been able to move past it and find peace in my heart. Nathan had not yet been able to come to that point.

Weeks turned into months. I began to feel a strong burden to pray. I prayed for reconciliation. I prayed for strength for Nathan—that he would be able to cross over and seek reconciliation. Whenever I am in a hard spot, I sure do count on the prayers of the people who love me.

Nathan's heart seemed to remain the same. And one day, months after the event, I was thinking and wondering if it would ever land in a good place.

My husband loves cookies. One Saturday I decided to make some snickerdoodle cookies. It was my grandma's recipe. Sometimes our creative God wants to give us things to do in the process of answering our prayers. I have come to learn there are parts that only He can do, and then there are parts that are our responsibility.

Let me give you some biblical examples.

In Matthew chapter fourteen we find the miracle of the feeding of the five thousand. What did Jesus ask for? He asked for the five loaves and two fish. He received something very small and insignificant, and then He added to it His miraculous power to marvelously feed over five thousand people.

In Exodus chapter fourteen, we read that Moses had to stretch out his hands over the Red Sea before the Lord parted the waters to allow the people to walk across on dry ground.

Then in John chapter two we read about Jesus turning the water into wine. What did the servants have to do before that miracle occurred? They were asked to fill the empty vessels with water.

Get my point? There are numerous other biblical stories where a person was given something to do, then God faithfully did what only He could do. God desires to partner with us as He builds His kingdom on earth. Understanding this idea of partnership with God will help us as we listen and follow His lead in our life.

So, are you ready for the rest of the story?

I followed my grandma's cookie recipe exactly—except for one thing. I felt a strong impression to put a teaspoon of anointing oil in the batch. I always keep anointing oil around for use when I pray for people.

Sometimes I anoint rooms of my house as I pray for a family member. I see oil as a symbol of God's presence. It was used in the Old Testament for the consecration of things. I have adopted the practice of sometimes using anointing oil when I am praying for people. It is something I occasionally feel led to do.

So in that case, I made the cookies, added the anointing oil, and prayed for God to touch Nathan. I would classify it as an unusual act that God led me to do in that moment. It's not something to turn into a formula for anything. Each situation I find myself in requires unique directives from God's heart to mine as I navigate through my point of crisis and need.

> *And they cast out many demons, and anointed with oil many who were sick, and healed them.* (Mark 6:13 NKJV)

Later that evening, Nathan sampled a cookie. His very words were, "I think those are the best cookies you have ever made." Monday morning came, and I put a little bag of those cookies in Nathan's lunch. At midafternoon I received a text message from him. The text read: "Would you send me [so-and-so's] number?"

The number was for the person I had been praying he would be reconciled to. You can't imagine the instant thrill of my heart. My obedience to put anointing oil in those cookies, combined with the hand of God, caused my husband to experience a miracle in his heart! In all the months of waiting and praying, that was the first time Nathan had expressed any interest in making things right.

Nathan made a call. They had a face to face visit. Peace came. And the Lord healed my husband's heart.

Would that have happened if I had not made those *special* cookies? I don't know—maybe, maybe not. As I pointed out to you in Scripture, many times there are things for us to do (and sometimes odd things) in the process of bringing about change and miraculous events. I refuse to overemphasize the act of putting oil into those cookies. What I will emphasize, though, is that I acted upon what I thought God was telling me to do, and the miracle happened.

We want formulas. But there is no formula outside of loving God, hearing His voice, and walking in complete surrender and obedience to His Word. I have never put anointing oil in cookies again. It was for that moment and that moment alone.

The key to obtaining the solutions we need is found in maintaining and nurturing our relationships with God—and doing in obedience anything that God requires of us to release His power to bear on our circumstances. We must simply go into our relationships with Him, hear His voice, and follow Him through our fiery ordeals.

Concerning anointing oil, I haven't seen in Scripture where God either commands or forbids it to be used. There are times when it seems proper and right. For more scriptural references on anointing oil in the Bible, check out these passages:

Exodus 25:6; Leviticus 8:30; Numbers 4:16; Mark 6:13; Mark 14:3-9; James 5:14; Matthew 25:1-13.

*For the Lord will rise up as at Mount Perazim, He will be angry as in the Valley of Gibeon—that He may do His work, His awesome work, and bring to pass His act, His unusual act.*
(Isaiah 28:21 NKJV)

*He is the one you praise; he is your God, who performed for you those great and awesome wonders you saw with your own eyes.* (Deuteronomy 10:21)

## GOD'S WHISPER

My kingdom is otherworldly. My ways confound. My thoughts always bring reactions. My works will amaze or repel—according to the heart. When I act, motives are exposed, and minds can be offended. One who is walking in step with my Spirit will experience reactions of surprise and wonderment, yet it won't move into offense and disengagement with me. I know whose are mine. Those abiding in me don't have me in a box for their convenient theology. The ones who are seeking me with their whole hearts may still be cautious but are willing to "step out of the boat" and try some water-walking every so often. I give you moments of comfort and rest, but I also give you tests, as any good teacher does. I know sometimes you will step out, and at other times you won't. It's all okay. I am in love with you either way. Just understand there truly is more than your current experience in walking with me. I am gentle and kind. And I take you from the point where you are and go from there.

# 16

# Violate the Violator

There are moments when, all of a sudden, it's time to rock the boat and initiate an offensive action against the father of lies[23] and give heaven permission to embarrass him once again.

Present circumstances can swiftly become pregnant with possibilities of something else—something different and better than *what* is. But sometimes the possibilities are not realized because we are not willing to take action to see them birthed. And sometimes we hesitate to take action because the action required would appear too violent.

But I've learned there are times when I must violate the violator!

---

23 "He was a murderer from the beginning, not holding to the truth, for there is no truth in him. When he lies, he speaks his native language, for he is a liar and the father of lies" (John 8:44b).

There are occasions in my life with God when I need to roll up my sleeves and toss out the *passivity-security-blanket* and aggressively take by force what God said I could have.

The enemy will taunt and commit mischievous acts against anyone who is willing to lie down and take it. He may touch my circumstances at times, but he can't touch my stability and peace unless I hand it over to him. Our enemy works through people and situations to get me to come out of my seat beside Christ in the heavenlies. And refusing to do that sometimes requires me to walk out of my zone of comfort and go for that thing that feels foreign to my logic.

The natural mind does not comprehend the things of the Holy Spirit. I must have the mind of Christ. And with the mind of Christ I see that I can no longer stand on the sidelines and watch the spiritual battle. I must be in the middle of it and affect how it plays out!

I have another story to tell you.

As I told you before, my husband is a carpenter, and from time to time he runs into snags on the job. He was remodeling a bathroom, and that bathroom had a tile floor. There was a chronic problem with how the grout was turning out. Six times the tile man returned to fix the problem—and six times to no avail. It simply wasn't coming together as planned. It was a situation where you just couldn't quite put your finger on what was going wrong.

After the sixth try, Nathan got a call from the owner. The job still wasn't suitable. The grout work just wasn't coming together. On top of that, there was a film over all the tile from when the tile was re-grouted, and it would take an acid wash to remove it. My husband was disheartened.

What was going to be the solution? When would it end?

We were sitting together on the couch, and I told him we needed to pray. An anger rose up inside me. It seemed the devil was causing trouble on my husband's job. That wasn't acceptable to me. I began to pray and tell the enemy where to go! I told him to get off my husband's job and stop causing trouble for everyone! I told him his assignment was over, and he was not welcome there anymore!

I then said to the Lord, "Whatever you do, even if you have to send angels in there tonight to fix that grout, have mercy. We need help. Please do it!"

That was a very passionate, precise prayer, and I believe both hell and heaven heard (if you know what I mean).

The next day, the owner called my husband and said, "I don't know what happened, but everything is fine, and there is no more film on the tile."

What? Everything was fine? And there was no film on the tile? Yes! Well, I now know God's ministering angels can do grout work.

It was miraculous—absolutely miraculous. Quoting Hebrews 1:14, *"Are not all angels ministering spirits sent to serve those who will inherit salvation?"*

Yes!

We had some angelic intervention. And what did it take for us to experience it? First, it took an unresolved problem. Second, it took someone willing to take out her anger on the right antagonist (the devil). Third, it took God—who heard the prayers of His daughter and son, and sent help. That was a moment of desperation. It was a time when a miracle was just waiting for someone to reach into the heavenlies and grab it—with force!

*He disarmed the rulers and authorities and put them to open shame, by triumphing over them in him.*

(Colossians 2:15 ESV)

*I have given you authority to trample on snakes and scorpions and to overcome all the power of the enemy; nothing will harm you.*                    (Luke10:19)

## GOD'S WHISPER

I have purposed and planned for you to take territory the enemy now holds. Part of the reason you are living and breathing is to expand my kingdom and represent heaven on earth. In heaven there are no tears, sorrows, pain, or sin. This is your assignment on earth: to bring the good news of the kingdom of God—and to live and move and have your whole and total being in me alone. For in this place you will bring the atmosphere of heaven all around. The enemy of each person on the earth wants to steal, kill, and destroy anything he can get his hands on.[24] Your daily assignment is to abide in me and in my word, and to do my acts in the earth. Heal broken hearts and bodies. Open the prison doors of the captive. Spread the good news of my salvation. Stand upon the territory that belongs to you. My kingdom will advance through forcing darkness out. Light always overcomes darkness. Light always prevails. I have called you the light of the world.[25] Do not be concerned with the whole world. Simply focus on what is before you and how you can represent heaven in your home, at your job, or school. There is enough work for all. The more you are filled with my Holy Spirit, the more you will walk in the ease of

---

24 "The thief comes only to steal and kill and destroy; I have come that they may have life, and have it to the full" (John 10:10).

25 "You are the light of the world. A town built on a hill cannot be hidden" (Matthew 5:14).

my glory and power. All authority is yours from me. You are my child. You have all you need for life and godliness. You have my love, authority, and power to do all and take all that belongs to you. Righteous anger is good. It's possible to be angry and not sin. When will you be angry enough when you see all the havoc the enemy is creating in the earth? How long will you sit in your comfort zone? I have good things for you, my child. I will train your hands for war. The battle is already won, you simply need to go in and collect the winnings.[26] I have done what I have needed to do, now I will work through you. I choose to team with you in the earth to accomplish my purposes. I choose to give you choice. Love offers choice. Love offers the recipient of that love the power to love back if desired. I will love you if you choose me or not. I will love you just the same if you represent me or not in the earth. Rise up now, warrior of God, and do the exploits I have prepared for you.

---

26  2 Chronicles 20:22-25.

# 17

# Jump Off the Cliff

Let it be said of you that you didn't fail for lack of trying.

All my life I have sought to listen to the voice of God. As a child of God I am promised I will hear His voice. Scripture is full of stories about people who heard God's voice, acted upon it, and watched in utter amazement at times as God worked right before their eyes.

I have found that most of the time when God asks me to do something, doing it feels a little bit like jumping off a cliff. I imagine Peter may have felt this a bit when he was about to step off the boat and walk on water to meet Jesus.

In order for us to experience all God has for us, something must die. Our care of self must expire. Our fear of man must crawl up on the execution chair and take its last breath. I heard

Kris Vallotton say recently, "The dogs of doom stand at the door of our destiny."

How true is that? So picture yourself stepping over those dogs and into the next room the Holy Spirit has for you to occupy. Just keep saying *"Yes"* to the call of Jesus to go into all your world. Reader, may the fear of failure in you perish. Let it not be said of you that you failed because you didn't try.

Recently, I have been learning about the gift of the word of knowledge. In 1 Corinthians Paul wrote, *"To one there is given through the Spirit a message of wisdom, to another a message of knowledge by means of the same Spirit."* [27] In other words, there is a gift of the Holy Spirit that enables you to receive knowledge about something you had no way of knowing without God revealing it to you.

The Apostle John recorded these words spoken by Jesus: *"My sheep listen to my voice; I know them, and they follow me."* [28] I really want to know, in fact, what Jesus would do. He is my plumb line of spiritual activity. He came down here to show me how things are done. *His* heart for this heart-sick world is the same as when He himself walked upon the earth. Now, He has all of us who bear His name to deliver the message of the Kingdom.

I have two stories I would like to share with you now.

One evening we went out to dinner. As I was sitting there enjoying a moment with my husband, I began to hear some things stirring around in my heart for our waitress. I kept sensing she was concerned that her son would be okay. I also was sensing she shouldn't worry, and he would be fine. I felt I was to speak those words to her.

Well, talk about stepping out of one's zone of comfort! She came around a couple of times, and I chickened out. Finally,

27 1 Corinthians 12:8.
28 John 10:27.

it was check time. She stepped up to our table one last time to complete our transaction. Gulp! "Here I go! It's time to jump off the cliff," I thought to myself.

I spoke suddenly, "Do you have a son?"

The waitress looked at me and said, "No."

I was instantly embarrassed. "Oh boy, what have I gotten myself into?"

Then she looked at me and said very inquisitively, "Why do you ask?"

I said, "Well, I was just sensing for you some things I thought were from the Lord. I felt like I was supposed to tell you your son is going to be okay."

The atmosphere suddenly felt charged.

She proceeded to explain that she had three handicapped brothers and thought about it all the time. She continually wondered if her child would be okay if or when she had a son.

Instantly we both teared up. I told her God loves her so much that He wanted her to know she didn't have to worry about that anymore.

She stepped back saying she thought she was going to cry.

I believe she did go in the back and have a moment. We looked for her when we left, and she was nowhere to be found.

That experience rattled me to the core. I wondered what God had just used me to do? I had been desiring to hear Him better. That bit of knowledge that God shared with me at the restaurant caused me to be in a state of awe. God wanted to speak to that gal about a child who wasn't even in existence yet. He wanted to help her with her fear of having a disabled son.

The one thing that struck me was that I don't always have the correct interpretation for what God is showing me. I thought she had a son. She didn't. The word of knowledge I received in its pure-given form was this: "Her son is going to be fine." I am learning to just stick with the organic word or phrase God gives to me.

When we hear from God and follow His prompting (no matter how embarrassing it might turn out for us), we have the possibility of bringing the hope of heaven to our pain-filled world. I tasted something that night I had never tasted before (at least to that level). I spoke to a perfect stranger about something I didn't know—but God knew. I overcame my fears, and God used me to deal with someone else's fears.

Wow! We have been given the ministry of reconciliation.[29] This means our job is to bring heaven to earth and connect souls to the heart of God in our daily interaction with people.

Here is another story of a word of knowledge in action:

I have been part of a monthly outreach in one of our local parks. Several of us gather on the third Saturday of each month and bring things to give out (food, clothes, school supplies, and so forth). We share the gospel message, sing and worship, play games with the children, and pray for folks in need of prayer.

One particular afternoon my friend had just shared a message of encouragement to all who were gathered around. Then the Holy Spirit dropped this phrase into my heart: "Someone is having pain in his arm." I didn't hesitate but quickly spoke out and asked if there was anyone there who was having arm pain. A man said, "Yes."

He was having pain in his elbow and shoulder. He was also having trouble raising his arm. A couple of us gathered around him, and with his permission, we started praying and speaking to the pain to leave his body. In a moment, the man was set free of all pain and had 100% range-of-motion return to his arm. Praise God!

---

29 2 Corinthians 5:18.

My *jump-off-the-cliff* moment was blurting out, "Is there anyone who is having pain in his arm?"

"What if no one is having pain in his arm?" I thought, "What will I look like?"

Friend, we must learn to smother the fear of man and step over the dogs of doom that sit at the door of our destiny! And in order for people to be delivered from their fears as I minister to them, at times I must snuff out my own fear.

On another occasion I was with a prayer team. We were praying for a man I did not know. The Lord gave me the phrase, "reoccurring dreams." I asked the man if he had been having reoccurring dreams. He said, "Yes."

He said the dream was of a time in the past when he found his wife in bed with another man. They separated, but he was having nightmares of that traumatic event every night. It had turned into a nightly bad dream he just couldn't shake. We prayed for him that night. God wanted to touch him and stop the torment. Months later I inquired through a mutual friend who knew the man if the bad dreams had stopped. And they had.

Our assignment is to connect people with the love of God. How will we do this? We will do it the same way Jesus did. He only did what He saw His Father do.[30] And now we simply need to do what Jesus did—and still does—through the ministry of the Holy Spirit. Doing this requires us to have a deep relationship with the Holy Spirit. And doing this will require us to put into practice what He reveals to us. We must listen for His voice and learn what His voice sounds like.

You *can* hear God's voice. The Bible says so.[31] I encourage you to take times in your day to write out your prayers and desires to God, then listen. You will hear Him—I promise. He wants to talk

30 John 5:19.
31 "My sheep listen to my voice; I know them, and they follow me" (John 10:27).

to you more than you even want to talk to Him! Read your Bible every day. Hide God's Word in your heart. The Holy Spirit will draw upon what you have hidden in your heart.

The enemy wants you to believe you cannot hear God's voice. Silence his lie, and dig into what belongs to you in Jesus' name!

I am stirred to expect the unexpected and to follow His lead. Will I make mistakes? Probably. Will it be worth it? Absolutely!

*The people that do know their God shall be strong, and do exploits.* (Daniel 11:32b KJV)

## GOD'S WHISPER

The place of influence is usually the place of death. Unless a grain of wheat falls to the earth and dies, it bears no fruit.[32] Death to your pride, death to your desire, death to fear and worry. The way forward may feel like a backward motion, but I promise you the path to life involves death. You cannot have it both ways, child. You cannot have all of me and all of you at the same time. It simply doesn't mix. Do water and oil mix? No. Neither do two different wills. Either *my will* will die in you or *your will* will die in you. One will live, and one will die. You get to choose. You always get to choose what your harvest will look like. Will you always choose what feels safe and comfortable? If so, then your life will be boring and predictable. Comfort-zone living is the enemy of Kingdom-zone living. To walk with me means your natural senses will be offended at times. To have all I want for you means your logic and reason must be denied at times. To live and move and have your being in me will create offense

---

32 John 12:24.

in others at times. In order to live your life by the Holy Spirit, others will misunderstand you at times. But on the other hand, the impact and influence you will have with others on behalf of the Kingdom of God will astound you and create a wonder and awe you have never known. Just think of the expanse of the universe. It's unending. So it is in the life of the one dead to self. The spiritual expanse and realm of possibilities are inexhaustible. Just as a rocket goes into the sky to explore what is out there, be my rocket, and let me fuel you into the realm of the unknown. Yet, is it unknown to *me*? No, it is not! Dare to believe impossibilities. Let go of reason and logic in exchange for faith and trust. I will teach you how to break the spiritual sound barrier and create through you such impact and discovery. Souls depend on your actions of faith and trust. When you speak for me, I will fill your mouth as you open it to encourage and help another. Think about these things, my beloved. They are words of life that will bear fruit that will remain if you choose to enter into new places with me.

# 18

# Three Times, Three Days, Three Years

How can we, who live in the natural realm, come into relationship with God, who lives in the supernatural realm? There's only one possibility. The supernatural must invade the natural. The natural says, "Yes, there must be a collision. The possible must touch the impossible." Faith is the bridge between what is and what God wants to do. He calls me, and I respond in faith. It's the story of the Lover calling to the loved. It's a testimony of the loved, saying, "Yes," over and over again. That, my friend, is how we become friends with God.

In the summer of 1991, Nathan was laid off from his job. He signed up for unemployment. The conditions of the unemployment stated he had to go to four businesses per week and have them sign a document proving that he had been seeking employment with their companies.

In the first week, as he got out of the car at the first business, the Lord spoke to Nathan, saying, "You will either trust me or you won't."

Nathan said to the Lord, "I do trust you." Nathan then proceeded to walk into the first business office.

When he got out of his car at the second place, the Lord spoke again those same words. "You will either trust me or you won't."

Nathan said once more, "I do trust you."

After that second encounter, Nathan found a phone booth and called me (those were pre-cell-phone days). He told me he was going to cancel his unemployment claim and just trust the Lord to provide. He asked me if I was okay with that, and I told him I was.

Nathan then went to the unemployment office, canceled his claim, and went home.

That night at church, a man came up to Nathan and told him he felt impressed of the Lord to tell him something. He then proceeded to say to Nathan, "You will either trust me or you won't."

It was, verbatim, what God had spoken to Nathan not once but twice earlier that day—and now a third time. Nathan thanked the man and told him he did trust God.

When we got home from church that evening, the phone rang. It was a man we did not know. He asked Nathan if he was willing and able to build a porch for him. Nathan told him he could. The man then told Nathan he needed it ready in three days. Nathan told him he could be there first thing the next morning.

Nathan built the porch and finished it just in time.

When Nathan got home from finishing that job, the phone rang, and it was someone else asking if he could start a job right away. For the next three years, no two jobs ever overlapped. As soon as Nathan finished one job, a call came from someone asking him to take on the next job.

Could it be that each of the three years was linked to the three times God asked Nathan if he trusted him? Possibly.

*When they had finished eating, Jesus said to Simon Peter, "Simon son of John, do you love me more than these?"*

*"Yes, Lord," he said, "you know that I love you."*

*Jesus said, "Feed my lambs."*

*Again Jesus said, "Simon son of John, do you love me?"*

*He answered, "Yes, Lord, you know that I love you."*

*Jesus said, "Take care of my sheep."*

*The third time he said to him, "Simon son of John, do you love me?"*

*Peter was hurt because Jesus asked him the third time, "Do you love me?" He said, "Lord, you know all things; you know that I love you."*

*Jesus said, "Feed my sheep.*                    (John 21:15-17)

## GOD'S WHISPER

Step out My Child. There is life beyond the veil of what you know and are familiar with. Don't allow the familiar to rob you of the miraculous. There is more to what you comprehend in this minute. I have sights to show you, and glory to pour all over you! I desire to share the pleasure at my right hand with you. I desire relationship and communion with you in ways that will satisfy your soul and fill your heart with joy. Look up now. See my outstretched hand. We have action to take together in the earth that will advance my kingdom. Lives are calling from their cells of bondage. I want to take you to them, and you will unlock their prison doors with the keys I have placed in your hand. Step out, and the waters will part. Go into the fire, and you will not be burnt. Speak to the dry bones, and they will live. Touch the sick, and they will recover. Nighttime will come soon enough when the work on earth will transition into eternity. Now it is day, and I have made you the light of the world. Go and do according to my will. Our union of love will touch many.

# 19

# Gold Dust Wonder

I will never apologize for the creative ways God chooses to work. At times God offends the mind to expose unbelief. We must read the stories in our Bible—believing for our own mind-blowing accounts of His goodness toward us. He wants us out of our box of *rational* thinking.

Nathan hurt his back at work. An MRI revealed three herniated disks, two bulging disks, and one protrusion. The chiropractor sent Nathan to a neurosurgeon, who following examination recommended surgery. Nathan did not want surgery. But for two weeks, Nathan couldn't work and could do nothing but lay on the floor.

I had attended some camp meetings in Ashland, Virginia. Calvary Pentecostal Campground had become a place near and dear to my heart. It was a three-hour drive to the northeast of where we lived. All in all, I traveled to that amazing, glorious, humble campground six or seven times over the course of three or four years.

At the camp meetings a person could stay for free, receive two hearty meals a day, and literally fellowship with the world. There were morning and evening meetings with classes of all kinds in between. When offering time came, it was easy to bless that community of believers who had a deep heart for the advancement of the Kingdom of God on earth. The experience of those days literally catapulted me into deeper dimensions and understanding of the love of God and the supernatural realm that surrounds all of us.

That campground was and continues to be a hub of supernatural, Holy Spirit activity. On my frequent visits, there were always people from many countries, who had come for the same reason: to get a drink from the living waters of God. One time I was there, over thirty countries were represented in attendance.

Ruth Heflin was the director of the camp. She died in 2000. During her forty years of ministry, her burden for Israel and evangelism took her around the world. It was said of her that she preached the gospel in every nation before her death. She wrote seven books about the glory of God.

Ruth Heflin was a descendant of the eighteenth-century revivalist, Jonathan Edwards. And she became a central figure in what is called the *gold dust revival*. Some people who went to that humble campground where she ministered shared testimonies of gold dust appearing on their faces and hands. Some reported that God put gold fillings in their teeth. And some even testified of having seen diamonds, rubies, or feathers appearing in the meetings.

Does this sound extra-biblical? Remember these stories:

Peter was told by Jesus to go to the sea and open the mouth of the first fish he caught. Inside its mouth would be a coin they could use to pay their taxes.[33]

God miraculously gave the children of Israel manna to eat each day for forty years until they arrived at the land of promise—when it immediately stopped.[34]

A chariot of fire and horses of fire appeared and separated Elisha and Elijah, and Elijah went up to heaven in a whirlwind.[35]

Elijah called down fire from heaven upon the waterlogged sacrifice. And that godly, miraculous fire consumed not only the sacrifice but also the stones of the altar.[36]

God opened the floodgates of heaven and brought down what until then was a foreign substance to the earth—rain.[37]

There are many other biblical examples of heaven invading earth in ways that boggle the mind.

What I am about to tell you will stir your curiosity and possibly even tempt you to be a bit skeptical, but I can only tell you the truth of our experience. I am going to talk about what I call a sign or wonder of God that produced a miracle in my husband's body.

One weekend I traveled up to Ashland to hear an amazing testimony and word by Silvania Machado. She was a beautiful Brazilian woman of God. I ended up hearing her speak a dozen or more times. She had been raised from her deathbed to life and health by the power of the Holy Spirit. Not only that, but what appeared like gold-colored dust or flakes appeared at times in meetings where she spoke.

---

33  Matthew 17:24-27.
34  Exodus 16:4.
35  2 Kings 2:11.
36  1 Kings 18:38.
37  Genesis 7:11.

It was also said that oil came out of the palms of her hands. She collected it and anointed the sick with it—producing many miracles and healings. She spoke through an interpreter. Her basic message was always the same: *Jesus loves you.* The way she spoke of the love of God was always captivating and beautiful. I will never forget it. Each time I heard her speak, I was left with the wonder and awe of the love of Jesus for me.

As we worshipped in those meetings, the beautiful golden dust simply appeared on her scalp. She would step up to Sister Ruth's open Bible on the pulpit, run her fingers through her hair, and down came a golden glory-substance. It also appeared on the seats of the auditorium—and even on me at times. It was all over the aisles and stage. It was truly a sight to behold.

After the service several of us would take scotch tape and gather it up.

On one occasion when I did this, I brought it home to my ailing husband, who had been doing floor time because of his back issues. I gave him a piece of tape with the golden dust on it. He put it in his wallet and put his wallet in his back pocket (which happened to be the side where there were issues in his back).

The very next morning all the back pain was gone, and he went to work.

One thing Sister Ruth Heflin always said, which has remained in my heart ever since, was, "There is ease in the glory of God."

It's true. When we are living in the realm of God's glory, we will walk in an ease that is truly miraculous in the face of peril and trouble.

If you want to know more about the gold dust, I recommend reading the book, *Golden Glory*, by Ruth Ward Heflin.

This story reminds me of the story in Acts about believers taking handkerchiefs from Paul's body and laying them on the sick and seeing them healed.

*God did extraordinary miracles through Paul, so that even handkerchiefs and aprons that had touched him were taken to the sick, and their illnesses were cured and the evil spirits left them.* (Acts 19:12)

## GOD'S WHISPER

Would you allow me to offend your reason and logic? Do you think I can work in your life in ways that confound you? Do I have permission to take you beyond what you understand with your natural mind? The world thinks inside a box. My people should live outside this box and call others to expanded ways of thinking and acting. Love covers sin. Evil is overcome by good. Die to live. Stand still to win. Speak to those things that are not as though they are.[38] These are ways to think and act that the world doesn't get. Begin to open up your heart and put on the lens of faith. Faith sees before it experiences. Prepare the way for me by absorbing my love and desires for you. You are my arrow of impact in the earth. I will shoot you into the world each day, and you will hit the mark and expand my kingdom as you ready yourself for me. Let me bring my winds of change and discovery. You will be catapulted into places and spaces that are crying out for my deliverance and freedom. This whole thing is about bringing as many souls as possible into freedom and salvation. I will use you in unique and creative ways, dear one. Come on! Let's go!

---

38 "Therefore it is of faith that it might be according to grace, so that the promise might be sure to all the seed, . . . [including] those who are of the faith of Abraham, who is the father of us all . . . in the presence of Him whom he believed—God, who gives life to the dead and calls those things which do not exist as though they did . . ." (Romans 4:16-18 NKJV).

# 20

# He Makes All Things New

At any given moment the healing virtue of Jesus can flow through us onto another.

One evening my husband showed me his big toenail. It looked like something was wrong. The nail wasn't smooth like it was supposed to be. It was rather rough and discolored. I assumed it was toenail fungus, and I felt instantly prompted to pray. I put my hand on his big toe and commanded health to enter it. I spoke to the toenail fungus and told it to leave. It was a simple, yet precise and authoritative prayer that I believe the Holy Spirit gave me.

Weeks passed, and I forgot about it. Then one day Nathan told me I should look at the toe I had prayed for a few weeks earlier. To my amazement, new, healthy nail was growing out! His toenail was half new and half old. I believe from the moment I prayed, God touched that toe.

Wow! This simply never gets old or boring.

Think about something. Our compassion—mixed with our authority from Jesus—at times brings on the atmosphere for miracles to be released. I wasn't feeling anything extra that night I prayed for my husband's toe. I saw a need, knew God could touch it, and simply prayed.

God uses our compassion. Our compassion is almost like the vehicle God gets into when He wants to go somewhere. As I continue to learn and grow in my faith, I have noticed that I get to regularly participate in an incredible intervention of God where there is very tangible evidence of His actions on my behalf. Too often I flounder like the next person, but I also have tasted things at times that grip my heart so deeply and so profoundly that I know I'm on to something otherworldly and God ordained.

That, my friend, is what continues to propel me forward. I have committed to God that I won't stop praying and asking just because I don't always see results. I will continue to pray. I will continue to lay hands on the sick. I will continue to ask, seek, and knock!

*Ask and it will be given to you; seek and you will find; knock and the door will be opened to you.* (Matthew 7:7)

## GOD'S WHISPER

Just because you are looking at it with your natural eyes doesn't mean you should conclude that it's my perfect will. My perfect will is that the end of a thing is always better than its beginning.[39] Calculating your temporal, imperfect world without me is a great miscalculation.

---

39 "And we know that in all things God works for the good of those who love him, who have been called according to his purpose" (Romans 8:28).

When I speak, the realm of possibilities comes swirling around you with gifts only heaven can offer. Even when I breathe, the wind of wonder blows upon you with hope for your future. My nearness means that all things are staged for new beginnings and occurrences ready to confound the mind. I am the master of creativity and the author of thoughts never thought in your mind. Release me to think through you. Let go of previous solutions and answers, and step into the realm of new possibilities and wonderment. You haven't even scratched the surface of what my revealed intentions are for you.

# 21

# His Luxurious Love

His love is otherworldly. His affection toward me is fierce. The epicenter of His heart is my home base. The love of God is a foreign entity not found in this world.

It was a moment of truth. It was an afternoon encounter that has impacted me now for over twenty years. I had a vison, and I have revisited the vision many times in my mind and received instant comfort and strength from it.

When God reveals parts of His heart's feeling for us, it is meant to last a lifetime and beyond. Each time we reflect on what happened (how He did it), we can remember it and find the perpetual strength that He intended for us to find. It's something always available to us day or night.

To me, God's personal revelations of His care for me become the memorials I look to for encouragement and faith. They are like the places where the followers of God in the Old Testament set up stones to remind them and future generations of God's love and care. And each one becomes like the hotspots I touch on my smart phone to open up an application I need in challenging times—one that opens up a new connection with my Savior.

It was the fall of 1995, and I was in the middle of a huge shift in my life. It was a season of transition. We were preparing to pull up our roots in Ohio and relocate to North Carolina. I had never lived anywhere else. Ohio was where I was born, met my husband, got married, and had our three children.

A job offer came from North Carolina. We were at peace with the decision to move, but I was grieving. Did you know it is possible to have peace even when your heart is grieving? The part that made me grieve was leaving my home of thirty-four years.

My parents and my friends were going to be over five hundred miles away after the transition!

Did you know *transition* is the hardest part of a woman's labor when birthing a child? It's called the *transition phase*, and while it is the shortest part of labor, it is the most intense and painful part. It's the time of the opening of the cervix to the beginning of the baby's descent into an unknown world.

The woman's behavior may change during *transition*. There may be panic and disorientation. The woman can experience a plethora of emotions. It's in *transition* when she may ask for something for the excruciating pain. And something as simple as breathing must be intentionally focused on to help steer the advent of the new life about to burst into the world.

I was in a time of painful transition, and I experienced intense pain saying goodbye to my loved ones. There were moments of doubt and confusion, and we hoped we were making the right decision. It was my all-consuming time of thinking, "I'm leaving. I'm going to a place I have never lived."

I felt excitement of course for the new life that was coming, yet the new life had not yet arrived. Simply breathing and finding focus was critical.

I was at a conference one afternoon during that transition phase in my life. It was a time of worship. My life with the Lord at that moment was very real and precious. I felt we were in His will, yet my emotions seemed to be all over the place. There were fears, anxious thoughts, and all the emotions you might think of being associated with such a huge transition.

As I was singing and worshipping, I had a vision. I didn't see it with my natural eye—but with my mind's eye. I saw the Lord. He was standing with arms extended toward me. He had on a large, fluffy, soft robe. There were no words spoken. I knew He was inviting me into His arms for a hug. I went toward Him and into His arms.

As we made contact, I went so deeply into His robe that it was like I was completely enveloped, and I disappeared into His love for me. In His embrace there was warmth and softness like I had never felt. There was a holy exchange in that moment—my fears exchanged for His love.

I emerged from that vision renewed, refreshed, and fearless. I came away from that experience more in love with Him than ever. I received an infusion of fresh confidence and comfort. I was ready to move on into my new life in North Carolina, and a new memorial was set up on that spot that continues to provide faith and confidence to me today.

God's love is the most powerful agent in the world. One touch of His fierce love sends demons of worry and fear flying!

*See what great love the Father has lavished on us.*

(1 John 3:1a)

## GOD'S WHISPER

The very character of my being is defined by love. Love is the one factor that is shining upon you day and night. You are covered in my desire and fondness of you. There will never be a full exhaustion of my affection toward you. Think of my love as a continual feast. The nourishment of my love for you will sustain you through any storm or hardship. The presence of my love does not mean the absence of trouble. Yet the power of it is mightier than the oceans and deeper than the expanse of the heavens. It's the one thing you can consume and absorb into your body, soul, and spirit that will cause you to arise and soar just above the trouble and pain of life. Knowing and living in this love-realm with me will produce health in your emotions, and even in your body. It's the ultimate feast of charity and the fuel for walking forward and not backward. You are my betrothed. You are my sweetheart. And together we will operate in this union of love. I receive your love as well. It's a holy exchange of affection. This relationship we have is the most beautiful of all relationships. Enter into my embrace this day and at this moment. Enter in—again and again and again. Stop, feast, and absorb new dimensions of love prepared just for you now. For it's in the knowing of one another that our fruit will come and remain for eternity. As you live from this charity-realm, you can't help but influence and expand my kingdom in powerful and unique ways.

# 22

# Going Places

If it happened in the Bible, then it's there for my example. The
Scriptures are the plumb line used for guiding me as I step out
of my natural way of thinking and into the supernatural realm.
The grid used for laying out my Christian life is none other than
the written Word of God.

---

The miracle in the following stories may prompt you to raise a
skeptical brow, yet in truth, we experienced it not once but four
times over the past thirty-six years. Because there is Scriptural
backing for things like this, I ask you to study the Scriptures just
as the Bereans did.[40]

To this day, Nathan and I don't know why they happened,
but we cannot deny the fact they did. The following experiences
weren't even things we were seeking. They just happened!
Perhaps like you, what transpired is something that still messes

---

40 "Now the Berean Jews were of more noble character than those in
Thessalonica, for they received the message with great eagerness and
examined the Scriptures every day to see if what Paul said was true" (Acts
17:11).

with our natural brain, but since there are Scriptural accounts of similar things happening to others, we are comfortable sharing them.

After I share these four stories, I will offer you Scriptures in the Bible for you to search out for yourself. I hope you study them.

## STORY ONE

This took place in the fall of 1995 as we were in the process of moving from Ohio to North Carolina. Nathan had already started working in North Carolina. I was still at home in Ohio with the kids waiting for our house to sell. Nathan traveled every few weeks to Ohio for the weekend. One particular weekend, he worked later than he normally did on a Friday before traveling north. That meant a later-than-usual start in order to miss the rush hour traffic.

He got on the ramp to the major highway and found the ramp led into stopped traffic. He sat there for one hour. When the traffic began to move, he traveled only five miles over the next hour. Finally, the traffic broke up, and he was on his way. He calculated the five hundred and ten mile drive to see when he would get home.

Then, as he crossed the Virginia state line—what felt like a second later—his Ford truck seemed to him to be in the air like it was coming in for a landing down onto the highway. He found himself pulling back on the steering wheel as if he had control of the landing. Needless to say, he was extremely shaken! And just as his truck came down safely onto the highway, he passed the West Virginia state line.

Typically it takes about an hour to drive across Virginia. It seemed to him that he had just made that trip in a second. He wondered if he had gone to sleep, but he really didn't feel like he had. He drove on without paying attention to the time or the miles until he got to Zanesville, Ohio.

It was in Zanesville when he usually called to let me know where he was and when I could expect him. He looked at his watch, and to his amazement he discovered he was a little over an hour ahead of schedule. And when the trip was all said and done, it turned out the odometer was about sixty miles shy of what it normally would show for that trip.

The whole strip of Virginia highway was unaccounted for.

## STORY TWO

Nathan was running late to work one morning. The drive from home to the job site took around twenty minutes. He left the house at 7:49. He came to an intersection and checked the time. He was six minutes into his drive to work as usual at that point. Just then his phone rang. He glanced down to pick it up, and as he looked back at the road, he was passing a restaurant that was miles from that intersection. He looked at his clock again, and it was still showing 7:55. Five minutes later he arrived at work, right on time.

He made a twenty minute drive in eleven minutes.

## STORY THREE

We were traveling back to Ohio after visiting family in Pennsylvania. We got on the turnpike. I was driving. Soon we started a long climb up a mountain. We were talking, and suddenly Nathan looked and saw the water tower (painted like a world globe) that we always drove past after we had gone through a tunnel. He asked me if we had gone through the tunnel yet, and I said, "No, we haven't."

That was a trip we had made dozens of times over the years. It was a very familiar route. We then realized we were ten minutes on the other side of the tunnel from where we were just a second earlier.

We had gained about twenty minutes on the trip, and we discovered when we got home that the odometer was twenty miles short of what it should have registered.

## STORY FOUR

This is the most current experience of this kind. It happened in 2018. Nathan was doing a job in a place that was an hour's drive from the house (in light traffic in the morning). One particular day there was heavy traffic on the way home. When Nathan called me around 4:00 that afternoon, he said he would be home by 5:00.

I was very surprised when he pulled into the driveway around 4:40. I asked him why he was so early. He said traffic had been heavy when he got on the road. There was a bridge over a lake he had to cross on the way home. He crossed the bridge in heavy traffic, but the next thing he knew, he was miles farther down the road in a spot twenty minutes closer to home on a lonely country road.

It had happened again.

Just as I promised, here are some Scriptures for you to investigate and read for yourself.

*As the Lord your God lives, there is no nation or kingdom where my master has not sent someone to hunt for you; and when they said, "He is not here," he took an oath from the kingdom or nation that they could not find you. And now you say, "Go, tell your master, 'Elijah's here'"! And it shall come to pass, as soon as I am gone from you, that the Spirit of the*

*Lord will carry you to a place I do not know; so when I go and tell Ahab, and he cannot find you, he will kill me. But I your servant have feared the Lord from my youth.*

(1 Kings 18:10-12 NKJV)

*Now when evening came, His disciples went down to the sea, got into the boat, and went over the sea toward Capernaum. And it was already dark, and Jesus had not come to them. Then the sea arose because a great wind was blowing. So when they had rowed about three or four miles, they saw Jesus walking on the sea and drawing near the boat; and they were afraid. But He said to them, "It is I; do not be afraid." Then they willingly received Him into the boat, and immediately the boat was at the land where they were going.* (John 6:16-21 NKJV)

*So he commanded the chariot to stand still. And both Philip and the eunuch went down into the water, and he baptized him. Now when they came up out of the water, the Spirit of the Lord caught Philip away, so that the eunuch saw him no more; and he went on his way rejoicing. But Philip was found at Azotus. And passing through, he preached in all the cities till he came to Caesarea.* (Acts 8:38-40 NKJV)

I would like to also add that Satan can sometimes provide counterfeits for what God does. Think about Satan taking Jesus to the pinnacle of the temple and then to the top of a high mountain when he was tempting Jesus.[41] And we read in Exodus chapter seven how the Egyptian sorcerers could do some of the same miracles Moses performed before bringing the people out of Egypt.

Again, just to be clear, we were not seeking these experiences— they just happened! I'm the kind of person who says, "Why not?"

---

41 Matthew 4:5-11.

It is natural for us to be afraid of something we don't understand. I really get that. On the other hand, I refuse to put God in a box of *only-what-I-understand*. He is God! He can do as He pleases.

If I only accept what I understand, then I have reduced God to a person who looks just like me. God is bigger than my thoughts and imagination. Paul was directing his words to the Corinthians when he wrote, *"Eye has not seen, nor ear heard, nor have entered into the heart of man the things which God has prepared for those who love Him."*[42] But do you know what Paul wrote immediately following those words? He told the Corinthians that God was revealing those things to them through His Spirit.

That means there are things to see, hear, and experience that will be new to us. And things that others have not known are being made known to God's children. This means God wants to do things in our lives that we have never thought of. And I, for one, am going to give God the space He needs in my life to amaze me.

How about you?

*But as it is written: "Eye has not seen, nor ear heard, nor have entered into the heart of man the things which God has prepared for those who love Him." But God has revealed them to us through His Spirit. For the Spirit searches all things, yes, the deep things of God.* (1 Corinthians 2:9-10 NKJV)

---

## GOD'S WHISPER

Can the natural mind conceive what my heart wishes to do in the earth? Is it possible to gain understanding through pure logic of my ways and thoughts? I say, "No." I gave you a mind to think and operate in the earth. Your

---

42  1 Corinthians 2:9 (NKJV).

mind was meant to provide you with a will and help keep you safe in the natural realm. Your mind will not serve you well when you are trying to see what I am doing in the Spirit. It takes spiritual thoughts to unpack spiritual thinking. There is a crossover that must occur as you listen to me and follow my directives. I will reveal things to you if you are receptive to new and different acts and exploits. My thoughts will offend your natural thinking. My ways will oftentimes cause a stumbling in your heart because of the crossover that needs to occur. You cannot interpret what I am saying and doing with logic and reason. It must be spiritually discerned. When you are offended, it's a good moment to question that offense, because offense will derail you. My ways will offend you at times. Offense is an open door of invitation to dig deeper with me. Offense means something still needs to die in you. Not all things are of me. There is a counterfeit in this world, but you, who have my Holy Spirit within, will have empowerment to discern what is of me and what is not. You must discern by the Spirit, not by the mind. My Holy Spirit will search all things and reveal what you need to know. I will not reside in your box of thinking. I want to expand and astound you, okay?

# The Standoff

If we are to be God pleasers, then we must be faith walkers.

---

While working on this book, I have said to the Lord, "If you want to add any more stories to the book while I'm working on the manuscript, you may." And He has given me more stories to tell.

As I began to write at the beginning of January, Nathan and I had been in a type of *drought*. I currently work part time as a substitute teacher, and being a self-employed carpenter, Nathan occasionally runs into small seasons when there is no work. We happened to be in one of those seasons of drought.

He worked three days in December, and he worked three and a half days in January. Money was tight.

One thing we have noticed is that even when there isn't much income, we still have to pay the mortgage and electric bill! Paying December's bills and having money for Christmas expenses happened by God's grace. We had some unexpected refunds from the hospital, which allowed us to pay our December bills. Then January came.

We had been *'round that mountain* before, and it seemed God was permitting it to happen again. Nathan had money in savings for paying taxes. But he drained that resource to pay February's mortgage. We really had no more reserves after that.

The showdown commenced for the battle of our minds. Satan taunts and puts thoughts in my mind to get me to doubt the goodness of God. And I bow to him every time I engage in anxious thoughts. So I know that in every showdown I have with Satan, I must refuse and battle against his thoughts. The battle began, and my showdown with Satan became a violent standoff.

Here is a description of the standoff:

We had bills to pay. In the natural, we saw no way to pay. Then came the enemy whispering in our ears, "Did God really say He would take care of you?"

Nathan and I both had our moments of wrestling and pinning down those garbage-thoughts. "God has done it before, yet will He do it again?"

That time around we began to become more stubborn with the enemy. I heard God say, "Win this standoff!"

It was like a dog with a bone. We wouldn't let go. We became more and more adamant that God's Word is true, and the devil is a liar. The enemy offered fear, panic, anxious thoughts, worry, and sleepless nights in the face of natural lack. But God's Word tells us He will never leave us,[43] and all our needs are met according to His riches, not ours.[44] So we chose peace, joy, trust, rest, and all the fruit of simply abiding in His shelter.

I think we made the devil mad!

On Sunday we searched our house for any money around— emptying every coin jar—and took it to church for the offering.

---

43 Joshua 1:5; Deuteronomy 31:6; Hebrews 13:5.
44 Philippians 4:19.

It was an act of the *widow's mite*, so to speak.[45] It was an act of war against the one who steals, kills, and destroys.

That morning I was reading Doug Addison's daily prophetic words. He posted, "Things are going to suddenly turn around, and you are going to see miracles."

Nathan got a call from a friend about five hours later. They knew we were in a difficult place and felt the Lord tell them to call and ask us how much money we needed. A check arrived in the mail in a couple of days. God provided for us once again!

I then told Nathan, "I have another story to tell!"

As you grow in God, the answers to your prayers start in your heart in the form of peace, rest, and calm assurance that God will work out something—even though you don't know what form the solution will take. Then when it happens in the natural realm, it's simply a confirmation of what is already in your heart. That's what faith is. Faith really is the substance of things hoped for. It is a literal substance in your heart of hearts, which is as real as the blue sky above!

True faith creates a resolution in your heart that no lying demon of hell can penetrate. But Satan has faith in your doubt. Satan will stand toe to toe and nose to nose with you until he is convinced he has lost. Pure faith in your heart is hard-core evidence something exists that is not yet—but will be—manifested in the natural realm.

Moses won his standoff with Pharaoh. Noah won his one-hundred-year standoff with taunts and jeers as he built the ark. Joseph won his standoff with Potiphar's wife, who tried to seduce him (even though she thought he lost). Jesus won the standoff with the devil, who tempted Jesus in the desert for forty days.

That's the kind of faith we should all aspire to display. This is the Father's desire for His children in the midst of every relentless

---

45 Luke 21:1-4.

wave that comes crashing into the shores of our hearts at times. The Bible tells us Jesus came to rule in the midst of His enemies.[46] And He will do that in our lives.

Win the standoff!

Here are some Scriptures to meditate on as you prayerfully consider your state of faith today. I listed quite a few on purpose. Absorb God's truth. Marinate in it. Let it become bone of your bone and flesh of your flesh.

*And without faith it is impossible to please God, because anyone who comes to him must believe that he exists and that he rewards those who earnestly seek him.* (Hebrews 11:6)

*Now faith is the substance of things hoped for, the evidence of things not seen.* (Hebrews 11:1 KJV)

*Therefore put on the full armor of God, so that when the day of evil comes, you may be able to stand your ground, and after you have done everything, to stand.* (Ephesians 6:13)

*And Moses said to the people, "Do not be afraid. Stand still, and see the salvation of the Lord, which He will accomplish for you today. For the Egyptians whom you see today, you shall see again no more forever. The Lord will fight for you, and you shall hold your peace."* (Exodus 14:13-14 NKJV)

*Then the Lord said, "Behold, there is a place by Me, and you shall stand there on the rock."* (Exodus 33:21 NASB)

*And the Lord said to Joshua, "Do not fear them, for I have delivered them into your hand; not a man of them shall stand before you."* (Joshua 10:8 NKJV)

---

46 "The Lord will extend your mighty scepter from Zion, saying, 'Rule in the midst of your enemies!'" (Psalm 110:2).

*Now therefore stand still and see this great thing that the Lord will do before your eyes.* (1 Samuel 12:16 ESV)

*And he said, "Listen, all you of Judah and you inhabitants of Jerusalem, and you, King Jehoshaphat! Thus says the Lord to you: 'Do not be afraid nor dismayed because of this great multitude, for the battle is not yours, but God's. . . . You will not need to fight in this battle. Position yourselves, stand still and see the salvation of the Lord, who is with you, O Judah and Jerusalem!' Do not fear or be dismayed; tomorrow go out against them, for the Lord is with you."* (2 Chronicles 20:15-17 NKJV)

## GOD'S WHISPER

In the light of my Word there is a firm place to stand. Your natural mind will at times become offended with how I work in your life, but your spirit will thrive in my loving instructions to you. In your dark situations you need the light of my Word. My Word to you is the torch you need in your trouble. You will have moments of chaos and frustration in this world. The more you truly understand your authority and use the supplies I give you, the more your carnal nature and earth-tethered thinking will be lost in the light of my glory and grace. You will find your wings and fly above instead of crawling beneath the weight of difficulty. You can have it either way. I give you the choice of arming yourself with my Word or becoming entangled and entrapped by the mud-slinging lies of the adversary. I wish for you to walk in all the abundance I have for you. This doesn't always mean things go your way. What it does mean is your soul is out of reach and off limits to the demons of hell, who want to taunt and torment you. Hell wants you to commune with its torment. I have something much better for you. I have amazing moments to lavish upon you. I have peace no one else can offer you when you are in the swamp of life and all feels hopeless in the natural. The standoff is real. The victory is also real, if you choose it. Win the standoff, and you will fly and experience realms of friendship with me that you as of yet haven't known.

# Heavenly Therapy

Have you ever just been sideswiped by a divine touch? Keep hope, dear one. Stay positioned in faith and trust. The *suddenly* of God may just knock your socks off at times! God enjoys confounding my human thought-world.

---

Nathan has had back pain off and on over the years. I suppose his occupation has taken a toll on him. One night proved to be one of those times when it was doing that.

He couldn't get comfortable in bed that night. The pain was pretty bad. He kept waking up every time he moved. It was about 2:30 in the morning, and he woke up yet one more time. He was lying on his stomach. When he woke up, I (or so he thought) was giving him a back massage. It felt to him like I was using my fists, rolling them all over the center of his back. And the feeling of it brought him relief.

He told me he was about to groan, "the back rub sure felt good," when he realized I was lying there beside him, sound asleep! He then quickly thought, "Then who is massaging my back?"

Startled, Nathan turned over, and to his surprise there was no one there. He thought, "That was weird!" He then got up and started to walk across the bedroom, and as he did he realized his back didn't hurt at all! He walked and twisted around, yet he felt no pain or discomfort.

Nathan had a pretty physically difficult day at work the next day. That, for sure, tested the miraculous touch he received in the middle of the night. But he worked all day, came home, and felt great!

Again, there really aren't enough words to adequately explain the way God breaks through the mortal, natural realm and does things that simply confound the world of human thought. God simply enjoys touching the inhabitants of the earth. Whether you belong to Him or not, I believe it is the Father's heart to display and rain down upon you His compassion and mercy. From the self-proclaimed atheist to the most faithful servant of God, our Lord's love knows no boundaries or limits for all whom He has so carefully created in His very own image.

*Praise the Lord, you his angels, you mighty ones who do his bidding, who obey his word.* (Psalm 103:20)

## GOD'S WHISPER

Dear one, my love is exploding to all this day. It radiates all around the earth, yet not all acknowledge it or recognize it. The universe is held together by my love. Do I have your trust today? Did you know I am looking all over the earth, seeking whom I can touch? I love to *love on* my creation. Whether you accept me or not, my love and care expands to the four corners of the earth. It makes it easier and brings me pleasure when one of my own remains in a position of faith and trust. Posture your soul to receive all I have. Surrender your situations to my otherworldly love and care. I will uphold you and tend to all that concerns you. Wake up each morning choosing hope. Let your feet hit the floor in expectation of how I will move upon you and through you that day. Be infected with my love and infect others—those whom I bring across your path. Dear one, you are in my path. What does that mean? It means you regularly will notice good gifts come to you from your Father. It means just as those in the path of a great storm ready themselves, so ready yourself, because I am coming toward you in a fury of love—not to destroy you but to build you up and fortify you as you journey on in your travels with me. In this world, there must be tribulations to walk through, yet in the midst of those fires, you will find gems and sparkling treasures to pick up and carry—things that will be of great worth and provision in your hour of adversity. These treasures will come in the form of peace when your world is caving in. There will be diamonds of grace for you to use to forgive others when you have been wronged. At times you will find precious stones of stability when there is true cause to stumble. At other times you will come upon brilliant rocks of angelic assistance. I have much treasure to share with you while you are traveling the earth before I take you to glory. Oh how I love you, my dear! I gather you into my arms now. Let me hold you and warm you until the chill of your weary heart is gone. For My love is stronger than death and far surpasses any difficult day you walk into.

# Gift Cards and Grief

Hell does not know what to do with the straight-line love of
God flowing through us like a river!

For several years when I worked for the county as a direct care
staff member caring for adults with disabilities, every afternoon
we had *bus duty*. There was a small season of time when I had a
conflict with one of the bus drivers. For some reason she was
very contrary, argumentative, and constantly agitated. She never
smiled, and people could do nothing right in her eyes.

I told Nathan one evening how frustrated I was getting with
that driver. I then decided I would talk to her the next day. Dealing
with her was causing me much frustration with the whole process
of getting people on the vans and buses each afternoon. My fuse
was beginning to burn with impatience and negative reactions in
my heart.

But God had other plans for me that day.

During my lunch break I went through a drive-through to grab some lunch. Then I pulled into a parking lot in front of Kroger's. Christmas was nearing, and as I was eating there in my car, I began to have a strong impression to go into Kroger's and buy that cranky driver a twenty-dollar Kroger gift card. I battled the idea a minute thinking how frustrated and irritated I had been with her the past few days, but finally I got out of my car with the remaining lunch minutes I had and bought the card.

You see, forgiveness truly is the ultimate act of love. Mark Twain said, "Love your enemy. It will scare the hell out of them."[47]

I texted Nathan and told him of my thoughts and what I was going to do. Surprisingly, he replied and told me that just that morning he had an impression (which he didn't follow through with) to give me twenty dollars to give to someone that day. With solid confirmation, I nestled down into the fact I was right in step with the Holy Spirit.

You know what? You get to pick how you treat others. You get to choose if you are going to use God's straight-line love, which is raining down on you every second of every day. You get to pick offense or forgiveness. Our union with Him is what will separate us from the world. The sharing of the Lord's agape love will cast us onto another level of living, moving, and having our being in the earth.[48]

Out of our union with God will come a conception. The fruit of that conception is agape love running through me like a river. As my union with Him strengthens and influences me, all my thoughts, words, and actions will become marinated in His agape love.

Our love for God and people will be tested. It's in the heat of the furnace where our hearts melt into His and there becomes

47 https://www.azquotes.com/quote/616867
48 Acts 17:28.

no separation between our hearts. When things are as God intends them to be within me, there is no place to tell where His heart starts and my heart ends. There is such an intertwining of desire then.

I am at that time hidden in Him. And out of that beautiful union with Him, the supernatural occurrences and the atmosphere of heaven are truly known and sensed all around me. His glory is real and noticeable in my world.

That afternoon's bus duty came. I was determined to gently approach that miserable woman with the kindness and love of Jesus. I began a conversation with her by telling her how I wanted to have peace with her. I told her that I knew we all have bad days, and then I told her I had something for her.

Her reply stunned me.

She was a mess. In tears, she explained that she had lost three very close family members that year—including her mother. And she proceeded to explain how her grief was simply overwhelming. She bore her soul to me in a minute. I assured her of my prayers and expressed my sympathy for her deep loss.

The very peculiar thing was that I never saw her again.

I'm so grateful I heard the Lord tell me to bless her. Truly I would have missed a very important lesson in faith if I had not been listening. As I surrendered my offense and stepped over into the *blessing-camp*, I watched in utter amazement as the truth of my trial surfaced.

If I would have held on to my offense, both the driver and I would have missed a blessing. For light to break open the darkness, it takes acts of obedience to the One who is *crazy-in-love* with this world. We must let go and fly with Him.

I heard Todd White recently say in a podcast, "If you've got an issue with someone, it's not them, it's you. The gospel doesn't say deny your boss, deny your wife, deny your co-worker, deny your child. The gospel doesn't even say deny the devil. The gospel says deny *yourself*, pick up your cross and follow Him."

*Then Jesus told his disciples, "If anyone would come after me, let him deny himself and take up his cross and follow me."*
(Matthew 16:24 ESV)

---

## GOD'S WHISPER

Breaking the ice of this cold, harsh world requires abiding in me. There is a mountain to climb at times to reach the one who is shivering in grief and shame. To reach someone I am going after requires focus and sensitivity to my work. It requires a denial of the immediate in order to enter into the urgent. What is urgent in my mind must supersede all conversation and activity you are currently engaged in. For at any moment I could tell you to step over now. There is great truth to striking the iron while it's hot. For you, any time could be right. For me, it is not so. There is a fullness in time when I will have the greatest impact. After the moment passes, I must orchestrate another moment. I go to great lengths for certain things to happen at just the right hour. It's a sad day when I have the moment all prepared, and my dear one is too engaged in his own affairs. When there is no denial of self, I must forfeit what I needed to do in that moment. A soul is then lost in a cesspool of sin and a flood of sadness. Self-denial and surrender are tools in your belt that I need you to use every day. In our mutual surrender to one another there is a holy union every demon of hell hates. There is automatic shutdown of the dark realm when the light switch of our illumination is on. I in you and you in me creates a light that beams with high intensity and has a blinding effect on the evil one. At times my directives lead you up a craggy mountainside in order to set free one of my lambs caught in the thicket. When you deny yourself in full surrender and launch out in my plan, all of heaven is backing you up. The angelic host accompanies you, and the authority and wisdom you need swirls all around you. As you reach the lost one, I am able to touch that one with a glory-touch they will feel throughout eternity. For you disrobed yourself of *you* and armed yourself with *me*. That is a powerful place, dear one.

# 26

# Nighttime Guest

Angels are all around. They are our friends, here to
help us in our times of need.

Have you ever seen an angel? I haven't with my natural eyes, but
I have been aware of their presence on more than one occasion.
And others have told me they have seen them around me.

One Sunday morning at church, I had my eyes closed in
worship. Suddenly, in my mind's eye (eyes still closed), I saw a
very tall angel up front in the middle of the platform with arms
raised high to the heavens in worship with us. I then opened my
eyes. On the platform, one of our worship leaders was standing
in that same spot with her arms raised high to the sky in worship.
It made me smile.

One night when we went to bed, a couple of hours later
Nathan heard a noise at our bedroom door and opened his eyes.
What I describe next is what he saw with his natural eyes. He saw
a very tall angel coming through the doorway. The angel actually
had to duck down to come into our bedroom. His head went to
the ceiling.

Nathan described him as "glowing white." The room was full of peace, and there was no fear. Nathan asked him if he had something to tell him. The angel told him, "No," but he had something for him. At this point I am going to refrain from telling you what it was, because it's a personal story of Nathan's.

After the interaction with the angel, I began to stir and woke up. I was totally oblivious to the angel as I got out of bed to go to the bathroom. Nathan could not believe I could not see the angel. He began to wonder if what he saw was even real. Then something happened.

As I walked by the angel to go out of the bedroom, the angel bent down, wrapped his arm around my head, and with his other hand knuckled me on the top of my head—like someone would fondly do to his kid sister. Just as he did that, I lifted my hand up and rubbed my head, like I had just felt something. Nathan no longer wondered if it was real. The angel then turned back to him with a warm smile and disappeared.

The word *angel* occurs over 200 times in the Bible. I realize angels are a phenomenon that maybe has been over-emphasized, yet I don't think it's right to never talk about them. Of course we aren't to worship angels, but we should understand their purpose and thank God for His divine helpers. It was, after all, God's idea to create them for His purposes.

As I think of Biblical stories about angels, I see that some of their duties entail bringing messages (Luke 1:19), speaking to us in our dreams (Matthew 1:20), keeping us on track and escorting us to where God is taking us (Exodus 23:20), coming to our assistance in response to our prayers (Numbers 20:16), bringing destruction (2 Samuel 24:17), bringing food (1 Kings 19:5), bringing protection to God's people (Luke 4:10), delivering those who trust God (Daniel 3:28), telling people to not be afraid (Matthew 28:5), bringing strength (Luke 22:43), opening literal prison doors (Acts 5:19), waking us up out of our sleep (Acts 12:7), and on and on.

I only skimmed the surface of angelic activities in the Scriptures.

Sometimes at the cost of avoiding the subject altogether we have come to a plain disregard of angelic messengers sent directly from the hand of God to assist us. We have fears of appearing over-attentive to these divine, lovely beings. I say, let's just keep them in the bag of our mix of supernatural possibilities in our day-to-day adventures!

*Are not all angels ministering spirits sent to serve those who will inherit salvation?* (Hebrews 1:14)

---

## GOD'S WHISPER

My angels are here for me and you. I created them to worship me and help you. They are in my charge, and I send them to the earth and back for assignments and missions that are advancing my kingdom. They escort and travel with those to whom I send them. They are fun, and I enjoy these beings. Call to me in your need, and I will dispatch what is needed on your behalf. Don't fear them, and remember they were my idea first. It's okay to think about them and learn about them in my Word. Sometimes you might see one and not even be aware. At other times I just might open your eyes to see one. Let the knowledge of their presence help to settle you in your time of crisis. I have them serving you as they serve me. Whether you see them or not, I have given them to you to take care of you and stand guard. You will never know on this side of eternity how much they have been dispatched on your behalf. Get comfortable with their presence, and know that each messenger I send your way is there for a specific purpose. Angels help you expand my kingdom. They are servants to me.

# 27

# The Gift That Keeps On Giving

PRAY—**P**ossibilities **R**adiating **A**round **Y**ou.

When you go to God in prayer, remember, you are going into a realm of taking from the unseen world and depositing into the seen realm. This is friendship with God at its finest.

From time to time, because of heavy use, Nathan needs to replace his work truck. One time, his truck needed work, and the cost of repairs was beyond its value. It was time to replace it. But going into debt to do that was not something he felt good about doing.

He began to look for a different truck and decided he wanted a white Ford F150 with a manual transmission. He wanted a white truck because (in his words) "the good guys always ride white horses." One particular day he set up appointments to look at two different trucks after work. As the day wore on, he started feeling the need to cancel those appointments because of an inner sense that going into debt was not an option. He went home and headed for the *man cave.*

As he sat there in his chair, he began to pray saying, "When my kids were home, I always tried to keep them in a good vehicle. I am a son of God, so I'm asking *you* to provide me with a debt free, white, F150 truck with a manual transmission."

His secret prayer swirled around the throne room of grace. About thirty minutes later, the doorbell rang. They were people he knew. They asked Nathan to step outside to look at something. As he stepped outside, sitting in the driveway was their white Ford F150 that *coincidently* had a manual transmission. They said they were just in town, and the Lord spoke to them and told them they were supposed to come to our house and give Nathan their truck.

God is not great just because He takes care of big things. God is great because He concerns himself with even the smallest details of our requests. It was another holy moment in the Christopher household. Nathan inquired as to what they were going to do without a vehicle. They told him the Lord told them to give the truck to him, so it was God's problem, not theirs. A few days later they found a wonderful deal on another vehicle. And it all ended well for everyone.

One more note: After that provision, two and a half years and many miles later, Nathan sold that truck and replaced it with another truck for less money than he had sold the F150 for. And one and a half years after that, and even many more miles later, he sold *that* truck for more money than the truck he currently drives as I am writing this.

How often do we miss an opportunity to be blessed in our natural world simply because we choose to stay silent in the prayer room? I'm not at all implying God is some celestial slot machine we put our twenty-five-cent prayer into for a return of what we want, yet I'm also not saying to never ask God for something you need or want.

Think of your children if you have any. When they ask you for something, especially something they need, doesn't your heart simply want to provide it for them?

No, they don't get everything they ask for, but neither does our Father give us everything we ask *Him* for. But part of our relationship with Him is letting our requests be made known. God wants us to ask.

We make the request, then we bathe prayer with our trust in the One who loves and knows us best. If we receive what we asked for, great! If we don't, great! We know God loves us and will work according to His plan in our life surrendered to Him. It's safe either way.

More often than not, we enter into a season of waiting once we have made our request. In the place of waiting there is a big box with a red bow around it just waiting for us to open. Do you know what that gift is? It is the perfect gift of perseverance. As we persevere in waiting, we build strength and stability. Our trusting heart is our gift given to God as we wait for Him to work on our behalf.

*Be anxious for nothing, but in everything by prayer and supplication with thanksgiving let your requests be made known to God.* (Philippians 4:6 NASB)

## GOD'S WHISPER

I have answers, solutions, and gifts in my hand, ready for the one asking, seeking, and knocking on the door of heaven—if you only knew how often I stand ready to reveal the plan or place the gift into your life. The realm of what is possible constantly swirls around you waiting for you to grab it. Remember I own it all, and I give out what is needed according to my wisdom and love for you. Sometimes I simply lavish things upon you without you asking me for anything. At other times I wait for you to ask. Both ways of meeting your needs have a meaning and purpose. Growth and maturity recognizes there is something for you to do at times to apprehend all I have for you. I will always provide for you and help you. My methods might confound your mind at times, but there will always be a solution to your perplexities. At times you will need to wait, and at other times the answer is just as close as your next breath. The key for you is to learn to trust me in whatever method I choose. Long periods of waiting will be one of my purifying tools at times to bring to the surface an ugly attitude or mistrust you have with me. I am bound to reveal my love for you. I will and have taken whatever means necessary to unveil my passion and affections toward you. I want you to have what you need. I want to give you all that is necessary to thrive and be victorious. Since you know your natural world so well, I will be teaching the one who is looking for them the powerful keys to living that are drawn from the spiritual realm. It's a training. It's a beautiful mindset to lay hold of. The dimensions of glory I want to show you will be special and addictive to your soul. There are ways I want to connect with you yet untapped. I want to create more thirst in your heart to see me in places you have never seen me. I am all around you in your world. I am within you. I am above you and beneath you. There is no place you can travel or walk that I am not there. It will bring such comfort to your heart when you truly meditate on my alertness toward you. I am near, beloved, and I am swirling about you with songs of deliverance. Tune in to my songs over you. Have you awoken in the morning with a song of deliverance on your heart? Sometimes I let you hear what I am singing over you. Sometimes that song ringing through your soul is what I am singing over you. Never be afraid to let me know what you want or need. I love to hear the supplication of my beloved. As I listen to you speak, then quiet yourself and listen to what I speak. This is prayer in its finest form. Truly there are divine possibilities radiating around you continually.

# Supernatural Ice

When you step out and do something that is new and different
from your daily grind, and you think God is leading you to do it,
you are probably preparing the way for God to amaze you.

As I am finishing up the last few chapters, I want to tell you about
something that happened just over a week ago. We felt impressed
to begin prayer-walking our street. So we have been walking our
street and praying about things every day. As we walk, we simply
pray for things that come into our minds. We have prayed over
all kinds of things like marriages, sickness, peace, protection, and
so forth.

One day as we were walking, Nathan began to pray for
appliances, furnaces, and air conditioners to work well and not
break down. When you pray, you aren't always aware of what
happens later as a result of your prayers, but sometimes you *do*
get to see what happened when you prayed.

Last summer, our ice maker stopped making ice. Our
dispenser continued to work, though, so we just began buying ice

and putting it in the bin. The following day after we prayed for our neighbors' appliances, I heard a noise in the kitchen. Could it be? Yes it was! Our ice maker began making ice again.

Every day since then, it has been working normally. That night we were in bed and just began laughing at the amazing occurrence. It was so thoughtful of God to heal our ice maker even though, in our minds, our prayers were focused on the appliances of others.

If God heals broken ice makers, how much more will He heal broken lives?

Sometimes when you are praying for other people's stuff, you might just find a miraculous provision for yourself. It reminds me of this verse from Matthew chapter six: *"But seek first the kingdom of God and his righteousness, and all these things will be added to you."*[49]

Jesus was talking about how God knows what you need when it comes to food, drink, and clothing. In other words, He is fully aware of our physical needs. I am convinced that as we give priority to God's agenda, He, in turn, will see that our needs are met. We were praying for our neighbors' appliances and not even giving a thought to our own broken ice maker. You see, God didn't forget about our own need as we were seeking His kingdom for others.

I want to encourage you to not focus just on what you need. Let God focus on that. Set your sights on how you can expand His kingdom today. Ask Him what He has for you to do today. What need can you meet for someone else to show them the love of God? It's in giving that we receive.

What if you would start prayer-walking your neighborhood? What if you would begin to speak over the territory God has given you? We don't war against flesh and blood, but we do participate

---

49 Matthew 6:33 (ESV).

in a war. There are strongholds, structures, and strategies from hell that have been in place and need torn down, uprooted, and overthrown. God wants His strongholds, structures, and strategies implemented in their place.

Take your territory, my friend. Intercede. Stand in the gap between what is and what God wants to bring in. He has called you as an expander of His kingdom. He has placed you as guard over your land, to oversee the ones He loves, and to care for their souls.

The lover of your soul loves them, too. Many need to be rescued. Many need a loving hand to pull them up and into their rightful place of dignity and hope. You are that one whom He will use to do it.

*Therefore I exhort first of all that supplications, prayers, intercessions, and giving of thanks be made for all men.*
(1 Timothy 2:1 NKJV)

*See, today I appoint you over nations and kingdoms to uproot and tear down, to destroy and overthrow, to build and to plant.*
(Jeremiah 1:10)

## GOD'S WHISPER

Dear one, my winds of change are blowing over you this day. It's time for a shift in your thinking. As you focus on my intentions for the world around you, a curtain of provision will open, and things will be done for you in ways that are difficult now. I know this isn't a natural way to think. Yet do I ask you to think with your natural mind only? No. You are my joy and delight. You are why I came to earth to live, die, and rise again. I gave you authority to rule and reign over the territories around you. There are places yet untapped by you. There are areas calling for your intercessions. I desire your attention in order that I may teach you. There is glory for you to spread all around. I have given you influence. The evil one must be put out of your territory. What comes out of your mouth will help determine whether darkness or light will be allowed to remain. Demonic beings have assignments for you to cancel and declare the glory of God in their place. What is removed must be replaced with the new and better. I have empowered you to bless and chase out the curse upon your lands. Light overcomes darkness. Blessing overcomes curses. Joy overcomes sorrow. Faith overcomes fear. You are a gallant warrior. I'm proud of your choices and pursuit of my kingdom. Let's go deeper and higher at the same time. Yes, it's possible. As you are seated with me in the heavenly realm, we will make history together, dear one.

# Midnight Mercy

His creative expression of love toward me is an endless
wonderment to my soul.

That night we went to bed around ten o'clock. Nathan's back was
hurting, and he was in excruciating pain. Right before he went to
sleep, he listened to the song *I Need You More* by Kim Walker.[50]
He went to sleep and dreamed. Later he told me it was as if he
could hear himself singing that song over and over as he slept.
According to him, after a few minutes or so he was still singing it,
yet he couldn't hear himself sing. But he kept singing it anyway.

I know it is hard to understand, but the dream world
sometimes can't be explained very well in human language.

Suddenly in his dream, it was as if a loud speaker was turned
up with an amplifier. His singing became so loud, it shocked and
surprised him to the point that his whole body jerked in the bed.
He instantly woke up. And he immediately noticed he was pain

50  *I Need You More*, by Bruce Haynes and Lindell Cooley, Integrity's
Hosannah! Music, 1996 https://bethelmusic.com/chords-and-lyrics/here-
is-love-i-need-you-more/

free! What in the world? He got up (easily) to test his feeling. He twisted and turned, and still there was no pain!

After he explained it to me, I then said to him, "Pray for my back and get the pain out."

So he put his hand on my back, which also had been hurting. He said, "Devil, It's time for you to leave my house with this back trouble."

His right hand was on my back, and his left hand was straight out the other way. All of a sudden he felt an electric charge hit his left hand and go straight through him to his right hand. My back got really hot (that was right after he followed by saying, "Devil, I am a believer. I am a disciple. I am a son. If you don't think you have to leave, take it up with God—it's His Word"). My back wasn't instantly healed like his was, but over the course of the next forty-eight hours, my back pain subsided as well.

Frankly, at times there isn't much to say except, "Praise God!" God just does what He wants to do. All winter long and into the spring, Nathan had been having back issues. Sometimes I prayed and nothing happened, and he went to the chiropractor or got a massage for relief. At other times I prayed, and the pain left. Now we have this memory of no one praying for Nathan, yet he was suddenly awakened from his sleep by a jerk and was instantly healed!

For me, this is proof that God is creative to the core. He won't be put in a box. I am ever learning and humbled by His works. Whether I see immediate or no results from my prayer, I'm going to continue praying and trusting for my needs and dreams for my future. Any misfire is always on my side and not His.

These are stories of a mortal communing with the Immortal. At times the veil between the natural and the heavenly realm is thick, and my prayers feel flat. But at times with one poke of the finger, the heavens are opened, and anything is possible! This mystery—this wonderment, this fascination—has me captivated and at times breathless, and it leaves me wanting more.

It's my hope that our love story will be told over and over again, for "I am my beloved's and my beloved is mine."[51]

*Let him kiss me with the kisses of his mouth—for your love is more delightful than wine.* (Song of Songs 1:2)

## GOD'S WHISPER

The joy is mine to engage you with my heavenly activity. There will be moments of question and mystery, yet there will be moments of the exposure of my gracious goodness that will pour over you like a soaking rain. I love you, dear one. That is all that matters. Absorb it. Marinate in it. Study it. Reveal it to others. Take time out to rediscover it again and again. Let it line the walls of your heart and soul. Be energized by my love and healed in the presence of *Love*. Your identity as my son or daughter is critical to understand. For when you know me and understand our relationship, things will change on the inside of you. When you become solid in my affections toward you, you will never be the same. There will be a stability upon you and within you, which others will notice. The more united we are, the more comfortable you will be in the sudden, unexpected happenings of my Holy Spirit. Our union will create hope and a healthy expectation in your life. It's like a dance. I lead, you follow, and then we enjoy and become happy in one another's arms. The music of heaven is my masterpiece and love song to you. Hear me

---

51 "I am my beloved's and my beloved is mine; he browses among the lilies" (Song of Songs 6:3).

sing over you today. Allow me to kiss your pain and bring soothing touches to your soul. As you engage with me, so will I respond in kindness and peace to your searching soul. Move forward in hope, faith, and trust. I will surprise you with many good gifts! I will amaze you with my loving kindness over and over again. Be still now, and let me pour into you this day out of my great love and affection toward you. For you are my sweetheart, my love, and my delight.

# 30

# Tell Your Story

There is no story like yours. It belongs to you alone.
It's worth telling. Tell it. Tell the whole story, or tell parts
of it here and there, but tell it.

As I near the completion of telling my stories to you, I am on a break between classes as I am substitute teaching. I looked up on the wall of this English classroom to find these words written across the top of the homework board: "You are the author of your own life story."

Isn't it fun? Here I am, writing my own life story, and I see *the writing on the wall*, so to speak, confirming in this moment what I am doing.

What is your story? What has God done for you? Your neighbor might need to hear it. Your family member may want to know about what has happened to you. Jesus said we shouldn't hide our lights under a bowl.[52] Your story is like a town on a hill.[53] It's not proper for your light to be hidden.

One day I made a quick run to the grocery store. I had to go through the frozen food aisle to get where I needed to go. The aisle seemed dark. But as I began to walk down the aisle, I was pleasantly surprised as the lights lit up unexpectedly on either side of me as I passed each section. It was fun, actually, to know that, as I went along, light appeared. Simultaneously, I heard the Holy Spirit say, "This is a natural picture of a spiritual reality. All of my children, who are advancing my kingdom, influence the atmosphere around them like this."

Since we are carriers of His light, it would make sense that everywhere we go, His light appears to chase away darkness. We are to display what God is doing in our lives. We are a flashlight helping others to find their way. We are the lamp that brings light to dark places. Friend, tell your story.

> *You are the light of [Christ] to the world.*
>
> (Matthew 5:14a AMP)

> *Let your light so shine before men, that they may see your good works and glorify your Father in heaven.*
>
> (Matthew 5:16 NKJV)

There are so many other times when we've experienced supernatural provision and occurrences in our lives. I want to quickly just tell you a few more.

There was the time our one-year-old son fell, and both of his hands landed on our hot wood stove. Instantly both hands blistered. He began screaming in excruciating pain. We prayed, and within an hour his skin returned to normal. The pain quickly

---

52 "Neither do people light a lamp and put it under a bowl. Instead they put it on its stand, and it gives light to everyone in the house." (Matthew 5:15).

53 "A town built on a hill cannot be hidden" (Matthew 5:14b).

left. The blisters were gone, and no skin peeled off. It was a speedy, miraculous recovery.

There were two different times, and two different houses we lived in, where the front door was kicked in and the house ransacked—only for us to find later that nothing was taken. Or did the Lord simply replace what was stolen? Either way gives way to rejoicing!

We had vehicles given to us on thirteen different occasions.

Many years when it was tax time, we discovered that what we had paid out over the year surpassed our income.

We were on vacation one year when our family was young. Every penny counted in those days. Nathan was working at a hardware store, and on the last day before vacation, his boss had given him an extra fifty dollars for the trip. When we were in the middle of the trip, our transmission line went bad. Thankfully, we were able to coast the car down a hill right to a garage. Guess how much they charged us to fix the transmission line. You guessed it. They charged us fifty dollars.

When we were engaged, Nathan didn't have work. Since we were approaching our wedding day, my parents were beginning to get nervous. A friend told Nathan to tell the Lord what he desired in the way of a job. Nathan went to prayer. He wanted to be in the construction field, to work locally, and to make five dollars an hour. Minutes after praying, the phone rang. It was a drywall contractor wanting to hire Nathan. He offered Nathan five dollars an hour to start and told him the jobs would be local.

Nathan and I woke up one morning, and after talking, we realized we'd had the same exact dream. We dreamed the same story and were in the same setting where the story happened. I still shake my head over that one!

Nothing is a coincidence. Every step of every day of every year of our lives matters and is being observed by God. Every word spoken, every deed performed, down to the way we love or reject others, is calculated and measured out before God. And every acceptance or rejection of Jesus Christ will determine each person's eternal destination.

The way you process what is happening around you—and to you—is a great factor in whether you develop either a *victim* or *victor* mindset. The way in which you filter life is the rudder of your life's ship.

Those who are seeking God with all their hearts are going to notice the hand of God with them. You will *see* because you are *looking*. You will see things others may not see as you press in to know *Him* as the one aim of your life.

Experience isn't everything, but experience can bring the Word of God to life for sure! I heard someone say, "The man with an experience is never at the mercy of a man with an argument."

I think there is some truth in that. Works—the things we do—and the things we experience will not save us. We will be saved because of our faith. But as James wrote, *"Faith without works is dead."*[54] The things we do, and the things we experience bear testimony to our lives in Christ.

God is ready and willing to demonstrate His own faith—and His faithfulness in caring for us—through His marvelous, miraculous works. And as you put your faith and trust in God, there will be many works that you and God will share together.

> *I thought it good to declare the signs and wonders that the Most High God has worked for me.* (Daniel 4:2 NKJV)

---

54 James 2:20.

# GOD'S WHISPER

Speak, live, and walk in a way that there is no doubt you belong to me. I have given you stories. I have given you inspiration and courage. Tell the world the good news of my salvation. Tell them how I saved your soul and planted your feet in a solid place. Stability is lacking in the world, yet not lacking in you, because you are my house. I reside in you. There is always a firm place to step next. There is always firm footing for the faith-filled person. I call you to carry your light strongly and continuously. Men shall see your light from far away at times and begin traveling toward you. Sometimes they don't know initially where they are traveling to, yet I know. For I have prepared you for their arrival, and you will teach them what you have learned from me. They will be attracted to the light you bear. I give divine appointments to my children. No person who crosses your path should leave your presence unaffected by the light within you. It should be that strong and lovely in you. My love and light is like a magnet for those in need. There will be ones especially attracted to my presence in you. Take care of them. Love them. Nurture and teach them. I'm especially proud of you. I see your heart of love and service unto me. Continue on, faithful one. We are fighting the good fight together and winning the war. Your influential light in the earth at this time is accomplishing much in my Kingdom.

# The Bridge

Dear Reader,

I want to prepare you a bit for the next three chapters in this book. Think of this as a bridge. A bridge generally connects two masses of land. This *bridge* is connecting two parts of this book. Part one and part two are each unique, yet they are truly connected within this book's theme and purpose.

I have just shared thirty stories that my husband and I have experienced. To me these stories are like an appetizer before a meal. Appetizers are usually light and very tasty, but if I were to end the book here, this project would feel like an incomplete meal.

I want to share with you some things I have learned through the years—things that will put the meat on this book's bone, so to speak. I realize the stories above were probably an easy read, and you were able to turn the pages fairly quickly. That might not be the case for the next three chapters. And that's okay. Take your time.

Please allow me to go a little deeper in encouraging you. I want to help you understand how God has taught me to think as I face my modern-day giants. I will do that through the chapter called, *The Mindset of a Giant Slayer*. It's a close look at the familiar Old Testament story of David and Goliath.

Then I want you to understand that when push came to shove in my times of pain and difficulty, without the power of the Holy Spirit at work in my life I might not have done as well as I did. I might not have been as brave to be God's witness in my world. So I am sharing an encouragement titled, *The Baptism of the Holy Spirit*.

And finally, I know I would fail you if I don't address how God has and continues to refine and purify my heart through the suffering and difficulties of life. For this, I am including a chapter called, *The Refiner's Fire*.

Many times I find myself having to climb the mountain when it doesn't move when I speak to it (Mark 11:23). I continue to learn in those times. Like other believers, I am refined in the fires of affliction in order that my faith might become more precious than gold, resulting in the praise and glory of my Lord Jesus (1 Peter 1:7).

So my dear reader, indulge me and continue on, even if it feels a little difficult. There is still yet an incredible intervention of His holy presence for you to find as you continue on.

# Part Two

# 31

# The Mindset of a Giant Slayer

## AN INTIMATE LOOK AT THE STORY OF DAVID AND GOLIATH

A giant slayer knows how to move past the naysayers
and win the battle. One who wins, first wins in his mind. The
helmet of salvation upon his head fits perfectly because he has
rejected the lies of his enemy. His truth-trained thought life
fuels his every action. The standoff is real, but so is the
potential to cut off the head of every opposing giant.

There are moments when the adversary peppers us with his
machine gun of foolish thoughts. Those thoughts he fires at us
always oppose the way God has asked us in His Word to think.
When we begin to agree with the lies of the enemy, we empower
darkness around us. But when we begin to agree with God's

Word amid the barrage of the devil's thought-attack, we begin to empower the forces of heaven all around us.

As we are about to see in the Old Testament story of David and Goliath, the army of Israel was agreeing with the bullying lies of Goliath, which intimidated them and caused them to react in fear. But David came on the scene with full confidence in the name of the Lord and knew exactly what needed to happen to gain the victory.

I heard a friend say, "Fast the lies and feast on the truth."

That is how we engage our adversary. We can head him off at every turn by firmly having our belt of truth in place as we walk in the peace of the Holy Spirit. Truth will give birth to peace. A lie can only birth fear. Applying these truths is a good way to test what we are aligning our thoughts with.

What is the fruit in your heart—peace or fear?

My friend, fasting the lies and feasting on the truth brings us peace, and this is what separates us from the world. This is one way we should really stand out in the world. Our reactions to difficulty must starkly contrast with a worldly response to bad times.

Francis Frangipane—author of many life-changing books—talks about Satan's hour. He says when we experience *Satan's hour*, "It is a period when the restraining powers of justice and goodness seem to withdraw."[55]

Jesus experienced "Satan's hour" in the Garden of Gethsemane. He was all alone. Evil loomed and overshadowed everything. In the face of injustice, He made the choice to die and redeem you and me. With Jesus being our perfect example, He obeyed in the face of evil. He didn't bow to fear and panic that night.

If He would have, I wouldn't be writing this book.

---

55 https://francisfrangipanemessages.blogspot.com/2003/01/satans-hour.html

As I said before, Satan has faith in your doubt. Will you prove him right or wrong? You are about to move into your destiny on a greater level, and he knows it. He's calling your bluff. Rise up, oh you giant slayer! Chase him down and cast him out of your thoughts. Make a public display of his defeat.

You will empower whatever you come into agreement with. The only thing the enemy of your soul can have is what you give to him. All of hell and heaven bends an ear to see what gains the power in your life. Will it be life or death? Will it be hope or gloom? With what will your union form, with light or darkness? Which spiritual beings will you empower in your life, angels or demons?

What Jesus did through the cross stripped away the power of the one who was used to doing as he pleased in the earth—the devil. God openly disgraced him and his realm in a public victory procession that continues to this day through us.

*Having disarmed principalities and powers, He made a public spectacle of them, triumphing over them in it.*

(Colossians 2:15 NKJV)

Our lives should continually disgrace and embarrass the powers plundered at the hand of Jesus. We, as blood-bought children of God, are to parade and exude the aroma of victory and triumph. Jesus won the war. Now we go, gather the plunder, and pile it up to the embarrassment and disgrace of our toothless foe.

Now, let's get on with the study of one of God's true giant slayers.

Please read First Samuel, chapter seventeen in your favorite version of the Bible. I will be quoting Scriptures from the *New King James Version.*

I have found many gems as I revisited a very familiar Sunday school story. As I studied the story of David and Goliath, the Holy Spirit began to teach me some things I had never considered before. I want to share with you eight takeaways from my study of this amazing Old Testament story. Since you have just reread the story for yourself, I want to get right into it.

## EIGHT TAKEAWAYS

**1.** The enemy can be relentless in his taunting and bullying. I'm convinced Satan invented the word "bully." A giant slayer runs to the battle in faith—instead of away from the conflict in fear. A giant slayer will not cower to fear and intimidation. He knows, just beyond the standoff, the victory is sure, and the glory of God will shine.

> *And the Philistine drew near and presented himself forty days, morning and evening.* (1 Samuel 17:16 NKJV)

> *And all the men of Israel, when they saw the man, fled from him and were dreadfully afraid.* (1 Samuel 17:24 NKJV)

> *Then David said to Saul, "Let no man's heart fail because of him; your servant will go and fight with this Philistine."* (1 Samuel 17:32 NKJV)

If Satan thinks there is a remote chance to derail you, he will badger you until you give in or fight him. The Israelites let that Philistine bully go on and on for forty days. They were terrified of the enemy. When David arrived on the scene, though, he got right to it!

When the enemy *presents* himself to you day and night, how do you respond? I challenge you to stand toe to toe and face to face with him in the name of the Lord until you get the victory.

You are not the victim, oh child of God. Never act like one. You are a joint heir with Jesus Christ.[56] You have all authority to defeat the bully of your soul.

David brought to remembrance all the previous times he won in hand-to-hand combat with the enemies of his flock.[57] Could it be that he was being prepared to shepherd the flock of Israel? Had the time come to step into the next level of warfare? I think so. Remember as you win your battles, God will bring you into an upgrade in the Spirit, and with each coming battle you will find strength for the day.

Each victory prepares you for the next victory. The defeat of the lion or bear, now, simply readies you for the bigger battle you will also win. Keep winning. You're on a roll! God will never bring us to a battle we can't win. That's just not His style.

**2.** The fear and dread meant for us will come back on the head of the enemy when a giant slayer is on the scene.

> So it was, when the Philistine arose and came and drew near to meet David, that David hurried and ran toward the army to meet the Philistine. Then David put his hand in his bag and took out a stone; and he slung it and struck the Philistine in his forehead, so that the stone sank into his forehead, and he fell on his face to the earth.
>
> So David prevailed over the Philistine with a sling and a stone, and struck the Philistine and killed him. But there was no sword in the hand of David. Therefore David ran and stood over the Philistine, took his sword and drew it out of its sheath

---

56 Romans 8:17 (NKJV).

57 "Your servant has killed both lion and bear; and this uncircumcised Philistine will be like one of them, seeing he has defied the armies of the living God" (1 Samuel 17:36 NKJV).

*and killed him, and cut off his head with it. And when the*
*Philistines saw that their champion was dead, they fled.*

(1 Samuel 17:48-51 NKJV)

As soon as the enemy of Israel saw their dead champion, they ran. Do you ever give your enemy a reason to run away from you? With the power of the Holy Spirit inside, and armed with the revelation of the authority God has placed in your hand, the demonic realm will know exactly who you are and be intimidated by your presence in Satan's camp.

Isn't it interesting that the very sword that was intended to kill David ended up killing Goliath? Now let's look at what the giant said to David prior to being killed by God's man of faith.

*So the Philistine said to David, "Am I a dog, that you come to*
*me with sticks?" And the Philistine cursed David by his gods.*
*And the Philistine said to David, "Come to me, and I will give*
*your flesh to the birds of the air and the beasts of the field!"*

(1 Samuel 17:43-44 NKJV)

I see three things in these verses that are worthy of special note.

First, Goliath's overestimation of himself caused him to be sorely mistaken when he thought he was going to be the automatic victor in his tangle with a *shepherd boy*. In truth, Goliath turned out to be a mere *dog with a stick*. Our enemy is overly confident in every attempt to bring us down. A haughty spirit really does precede a fall.[58]

Thinking more highly of ourselves than we should is always an unholy attitude that will bring a guaranteed downfall. This is one reason the adversary will always fall before us when we confront him.

---

58 Proverbs 16:18.

Second, Goliath spoke curses against David, which basically had nowhere to land. In the book of Proverbs we read, *"Like a sparrow in its flitting, like a swallow in its flying, a curse that is causeless does not alight."* [59] The curse was hurled but found no place to land that day upon the friend of God. So it is with us. Curses may come at us, but when they find no place to land, they act as boomerangs that return back upon the head of our enemy who is seeking our destruction.

Let's call this *boomerang warfare.*

When one is draped in the *Armor of God*, there is no curse or lie that can land upon him or penetrate his blood-bought armor. David was draped in the glory of God that day. He had his *belt of truth* tightly buckled. The thoughts of God saturated his *helmet of salvation.* This is how I picture David in the Spirit as he ran out to confront the enemy of Israel:

> *For He put on righteousness as a breastplate, and a helmet of salvation on His head; he put on the garments of vengeance for clothing, and was clad with zeal as a cloak.*
>
> (Isaiah 59:17 NKJV)

David was dressed for vengeance. He was ready and full of zeal. He was in right standing with God. He knew the secrets of salvation-thinking. He was fully engaged in the Spirit. That is a true picture of our warrior stance. Friend, God calls you out of your worry-realm and into the warrior suit prepared perfectly for you.

Then third, Goliath invited David to come and find death. The enemy never has a truthful voice when he speaks to you. Satan is the king of counterfeit. Do you know one thing he is good at? He is good at projecting onto *you* what he sees God has called you to do with him.

---

59 Proverbs 26:2 (ESV).

Remember, he is always calling your bluff. In other words, the very thing you are to come at him with is the very thing he tries to bring against you. God has called us to crush the darkness and kill off every demonic intention around us. The only thing Satan has is words. He has no power unless we give it to him.

Jesus was given the authority to *"rule in the midst of [His] enemies."*[60] And He calls upon us to rule in the midst of our enemies and send out the invitation of death to the bully of our souls.

I love the following Bible passage in The Message:

> *Jesus said, "I know. I saw Satan fall, a bolt of lightning out of the sky. See what I've given you? Safe passage as you walk on snakes and scorpions, and protection from every assault of the Enemy. No one can put a hand on you. All the same, the great triumph is not in your authority over evil, but in God's authority over you and presence with you. Not what you do for God but what God does for you—that's the agenda for rejoicing."* (Luke 10:19-20 MSG)

Jesus never promised we wouldn't have to walk on *snakes and scorpions*. But He did promise we would be empowered to step on the enemy and find victory. We are not to gloat in our power over the enemy but rejoice in the presence of God with us.

**3.** Giant slayers filter everything through faith and hope. They do not fall into intimidation but, rather, are angered that God and His people have been defied.

> *For who is this uncircumcised Philistine, that he should defy the armies of the living God?* (1 Samuel 17:26b NKJV)

The Hebrew word for *defy* simply means to reproach or taunt. The mindset of a giant slayer will not allow him to take scorning

---

60 Psalm 110:2.

to heart or allow a fellow soldier of God to be defied. It will instead cause him to go to battle on behalf of himself or others. David, in truth, was an intercessor for his fellow countrymen.

One who operates from a giant-slayer thought life will always show up to fight on behalf of those weaker in faith. David never belittled Israel, rather, he just went out to fight. Never belittle your fellow soldiers. Just get down to business and win the battle that's before you. David saw Israel as *the armies of the living God.* He could have called them *wimps*, but instead he called them God's army.

Wow! That's a teaching on its own.

**4.** Giant slayers are sometimes persecuted by non-giant slayers. And although experiencing that can be difficult, it won't distract the giant slayer from his battle-focus.

> *Now Eliab his oldest brother heard when [David] spoke to the men; and Eliab's anger was aroused against David, and he said, "Why did you come down here? And with whom have you left those few sheep in the wilderness? I know your pride and the insolence of your heart, for you have come down to see the battle."*
>
> *And David said, "What have I done now? Is there not a cause?"*
>
> *Then he turned from him toward another and said the same thing; and these people answered him as the first ones did.*
>
> (1 Samuel 17:28-30 NKJV)

Make sure you don't discount another's faith. Make sure you aren't aligning yourself with the *accuser of the brethren.*[61] When problems arise, if you don't go into intercession mode (giant-slayer mode), you might find yourself in the enemy's camp cheering with the devil.

---

61 Revelation 12:10 (NKJV).

Here we see the beginning of David's giant-slayer story. It seems his brothers were operating in the same belittling spirit Goliath had. Wow! Badgering from his own brothers could have put an end to the story right then and there. But David was secure in who he was, so it didn't happen. David jumped over the first testing-hurdle of that encounter.

When those around are not offering godly support and wisdom found in Scripture, do we have what's required to take the next step forward toward victory? If we do, that, my friend, is critical giant-slayer living.

That day, David moved forward with God alone. Facing our enemy alone is not something we may like, yet at times we may find ourselves in a position where no one is offering us godly support.

I know this is for someone right now. You are alone in your battle. Yet, are you? I say you are not. Recalculate, my friend. God is with you!

**5.** Giant slayers have allowed God to prepare them and are ready for a sudden encounter with the adversary.

*But David said to Saul, "Your servant used to keep his father's sheep, and when a lion or a bear came and took a lamb out of the flock, I went out after it and struck it, and delivered the lamb from its mouth; and when it arose against me, I caught it by its beard, and struck and killed it. Your servant has killed both lion and bear; and this uncircumcised Philistine will be like one of them, seeing he has defied the armies of the living God."*

*Moreover David said, "The Lord, who delivered me from the paw of the lion and from the paw of the bear, He will deliver me from the hand of this Philistine."*

(1 Samuel 17:34-37a NKJV)

All of David's experiences while caring for his Father's flock were used by God to equip David with the confidence he needed for confronting the giant. Our heavenly Father would never send His child into a battle he couldn't win. That would be mean. He has given us everything we need for life and godliness.[62]

Never think any battle you find yourself in is unimportant or goes unnoticed. A surrendered child of God will sometimes encounter times and seasons of challenge for the simple purpose of gaining strength in the Spirit. With each encounter that David had with a wild animal, I'm sure he gained confidence and courage for the next tangle with an attacker. Remembering former battles won is like a fresh reload of ammunition when facing your current battle.

As David saw the giant and the fear-battered army, what did he do? He remembered slaying the lion and the bear, and he told himself and Saul that God would also deliver him from the giant. When you win one battle, God brings even more sure-footedness for the next, probably bigger battle to come your way.

The size of the current giant I am facing is never in the mix of how I calculate my victory. My natural view of my circumstances always makes them appear larger than they truly are. In an encounter with darkness, I will win with the proper eye gear. Just as special cameras and lenses are needed to see through darkness in the natural realm, it's no different spiritually.

Natural eyes simply cannot see properly in darkness. It's true. Without proper vision you won't do well. The Bible tells us, *"Where there is no vision, the people perish."*[63] David had the vision needed to save Israel from certain death and slavery. When the taunts of the adversary come flying at you, greet your foe with

---

62 "His divine power has given to us all things that pertain to life and godliness" (2 Peter 1:3a NKJV).
63 Proverbs 29:18a (KJV).

battleground vision—to see the enemy's efforts boomerang back to him, resulting in his imminent defeat.

David had allowed God to train him in seeing beyond natural sight.

**6.** A giant slayer knows his enemy always misspeaks. When lies are being hurled, a word of authority and truth is stirring within, ready to shoot forth from his spiritual slingshot.

> *And when the Philistine looked about and saw David, he disdained him; for he was only a youth, ruddy and good-looking.*
>
> (1 Samuel 17:42 NKJV)

Your adversary always lies. He is the father of lies. Remember that. He thinks he has a chance to derail you. He's taking a chance you will just run and hide like all the rest. The enemy regrets any conflict with a giant slayer.

Here's one way you can tell if the enemy is coming at you. You suddenly feel rejected, belittled, despised, ignored, or undervalued. This is what it means to be *disdained*. Since David just passed the *disdain test* from his brothers and countrymen, he was immediately ready for the next level of the same kind of attack. When you pass a test with your family and peers, you are ready to bring down—with flying colors—the lies of a stranger.

Many of us would be stopped at the first closed gate, but the mindset of a giant slayer can jump the wall of entanglement with those closest to him. If you can win it with your family, you will most likely win anywhere.

Dear reader, I am sensing you may be in a difficult time with a close friend or family member. I want to encourage you to keep stepping forward in love. Resist the temptation to feud on the carnal level, and stay seated with Jesus in the heavenlies. Refuse the flaming arrows by lifting your shield of faith in the One who is training your hands for war.

Pass the test, and be the leader of great spiritual thinking among your family and peers. Don't bow to their cheapening insults.

7. The name of the Lord is the defense of a giant slayer.

*Then David said to the Philistine, "You come to me with a sword, with a spear, and with a javelin. But I come to you in the name of the Lord of hosts, the God of the armies of Israel, whom you have defied."* (1 Samuel 17:45 NKJV)

We need to have a true and real understanding that we are defenseless without the name of the Lord on our lips and in our hearts. It's not us. It's Him in us and at work in us. How often have you addressed the enemy "in the name of the Lord?" It's a simple thought, yet powerful when coming out of your mouth while engaged in a skirmish with the enemy.

The enemy hears you, and you hear yourself. It's like establishing the foundation of why you will win. There was no mistake who David worshipped. There was no confusion over where David got his empowerment.

Here are two additional Scriptures to underline this point.

*All the nations may walk in the name of their gods, but we will walk in the name of the Lord our God for ever and ever.*
(Micah 4:5)

*The name of the Lord is a fortified tower; the righteous run to it and are safe.* (Proverbs 18:10)

**8.** A giant slayer will prophesy to the enemy and foretell his demise.

> *This day the Lord will deliver you into my hand, and I will strike you and take your head from you. And this day I will give the carcasses of the camp of the Philistines to the birds of the air and the wild beasts of the earth, that all the earth may know that there is a God in Israel. Then all this assembly shall know that the Lord does not save with sword and spear; for the battle is the Lord's, and He will give you into our hands.*
>
> (1 Samuel 17:46-47 NKJV)

What comes out of your mouth in the heat of the battle is a great indication of the condition of your heart. How you speak to God, yourself, your friends, and even the enemy, tells much!

Remember this: you need faith to walk in the conviction of what is true. You need hope for a confident expectation of your future. David walked in the conviction of what was true. He had faith. David walked in a confident expectation of his future. He had hope. Faith and hope are not logical in the natural mind of reason.

Is the Holy Spirit logical? To the natural mind, no—to the spiritual mind, yes.

> *But the unspiritual man simply cannot accept the matters which the Spirit deals with—they just don't make sense to him, for, after all, you must be spiritual to see spiritual things. The spiritual man, on the other hand, has an insight into the meaning of everything, though his insight may baffle the man of the world. This is because the former is sharing in God's wisdom, and "Who has known the mind of the Lord that he may instruct him?" Incredible as it may sound, we who are spiritual have the very thoughts of Christ!*
>
> (1 Corinthians 2:14-16 PHILLIPS)

My natural mind will always stumble over and question what the Holy Spirit asks of me. We have got to run our lives according to the logic of heaven. Worldly logic and heavenly logic are polar opposites. How different my life would be if I relied more and more on what I see and hear in the Spirit rather than my natural senses. Peter wrote about how our troubles come in order to prove our faith is real.[64] So the proof of my faith is my ability to live according to the Spirit and not my natural mind.

If we truly want to enjoy Holy Spirit-adventures and develop intimacy with God, then we will *march to the beat of a different drummer.* Your words should sound different. Your actions should look different. Your thoughts should be taken captive every day and made obedient to Christ. Your time should be spent differently. Your love should always be turned on, and your emotions should be your slave and not your master.

All other voices must cease to influence your heart and actions. God calls you upward. He is drawing you and calling you to simplify your activity. Slay the enemies in front of you now. Be the one who runs to the battle instead of shrinking back. The glory of God is filling the earth this very moment, and you get to be one of its carriers.

As the world and the naysayers sink in the mire of negativity and doom, we—as God's giant slayers—need to rise above and not cower beneath. We are the head and not the tail. We are above and not beneath. We carry the banner of liberty and freedom through the cross of Jesus Christ. We get to represent heaven on earth.

You were born to shine with the glory of God. You were created to count and make a difference. The shepherd boy, David, found out his God was able. It started with guarding his father's

---

64 "These have come so that the proven genuineness of your faith—of greater worth than gold, which perishes even though refined by fire—may result in praise, glory and honor when Jesus Christ is revealed" (1 Peter 1:7).

sheep. It started with killing a lion and a bear to protect what belonged to his family. He graduated from protecting animals to facing a giant who was taunting and towering over the whole nation of Israel.

The size of Goliath had no effect on David. The volume of the giant's voice did not distract him from facing his enemy head on. He had singled out the voice of the God of Israel as the only voice that would dictate his marching orders. He had cultivated a love with his God. He knew what it was to lie down beside still waters. He knew how to be seated at the Lord's banquet table prepared especially for him in the presence of his enemies.[65]

The ancient, holy secrets of warfare were lining the walls of his heart. He learned early on not to fear evil, because he lived in the presence of the Almighty.

This is the mindset of a giant slayer.

*Then the children of Israel returned from chasing the Philistines, and they plundered their tents.* (1 Samuel 17:53 NKJV)

---

## GOD'S WHISPER

Leadership in the Holy Spirit is powerful. When you ignore the taunting and don't cower in fear and intimidation, you will attract attention on all fronts. I am looking for those in my house to train and mentor others to slay giants. Modern day giants exist. As fearful men witness fearless men, it puts a seed of faith and hope inside. When my sons and daughters understand the authority I have given them and know how to use it, it will awaken those slumbering in fear and dread. Fear and dread belong on the head of your adversary. Power and

---

65 Psalm 23.

authority are upon your head. As you learn to use your *war gear*, you will rise above and not be beneath. You will soar in the storm instead of sag in a slump of despair. You are a forerunner, my beloved. Take the Word and wield it in your hand. Use the sword to go into the offensive mode. Let your adversary find you in his camp dressed for war. I tell you, I have given you the victory, but you must take the position of victor and not cower. Battles will be won in many different ways. The huge way is in your mind first. The battlefield is between your ears! If you take it there, no storm, fire, or flood will overtake you. Yes, you still may experience pain and difficulty, but it will not wipe you out and take you down. Learn to use your sword. For the sword is my Word to you. If you are unaware of what I am saying, you are powerless to go on the offensive. Put on my armor. I give it to you to win and find protection. Be strong, dear one, in the power of my might. For in my might you will find shelter and protection. I call you my giant slayer. You are my leader. Others who are more cowardly are watching you. Rise up, oh warrior of God. There are battles for you to win and people for you to free.

## QUESTIONS TO PONDER

What emotion or thought do I need to master?

Why is it difficult to trust the Lord in certain circumstances?

Where is God calling me to grow and how will that happen?

What Bible verse can I stand on when the lies start coming at me?

Do I have a giant-slayer mentality?

# The Baptism of the Holy Spirit

## WHY THE POWER THAT CAME AT PENTECOST IS STILL NEEDED TODAY

After I was baptized in the Holy Spirit, it was as though my life with God transformed from black and white to Technicolor. Bible reading came alive, and I was more conscious of my mission—to be His witness in the earth. The ability to pray and worship in tongues has been life-altering.

*As for me, I baptize you with water for repentance, but He who is coming after me is mightier than I, and I am not fit to remove His sandals; He will baptize you with the Holy Spirit and fire.* (Matthew 3:11 NASB)

*And he was preaching, and saying, "After me One is coming who is mightier than I, and I am not fit to stoop down and untie the thong of His sandals. I baptized you with water; but He will baptize you with the Holy Spirit."* (Mark 1:7-8 NASB)

*John answered and said to them all, "As for me, I baptize you with water; but One is coming who is mightier than I, and I am not fit to untie the thong of His sandals; He will baptize you with the Holy Spirit and fire."* (Luke 3:16 NASB)

*I did not recognize Him, but He who sent me to baptize in water said to me, "He upon whom you see the Spirit descending and remaining upon Him, this is the One who baptizes in the Holy Spirit."* (John 1:33 NASB)

I find it interesting that all four gospel writers include what John the Baptist said about Jesus baptizing us with the Holy Spirit. To me, that's God saying, "This is one of the things I really want you to get."

John the Baptist also said, *"Behold the Lamb of God who takes away the sins of the world."*[66] So John the Baptist said two really important things about Jesus. Here's what we can glean from his words: Jesus brings to us two things—*salvation* and the *baptism of the Holy Spirit*.

God handpicked John to prepare the way and speak of Jesus. The simplicity of John's message exemplifies what our message should include as we also prepare the way of the Lord in our world today. John's message in a nutshell is: Jesus brings salvation, and for those who receive salvation, there is power available to be a witness of salvation.

I'm not here to argue. I'm okay with you disagreeing with me. In the end, I will be responsible for how I interpreted Scripture, and so will you. I simply want to attempt to share my convictions

---

66 John 1:29.

based on how I have understood and experienced Scripture. I have no formulas, but I have discovered that God wants to empower His saints to do what He told them to do.

Whatever you have come to believe about the baptism of the Holy Spirit, I pray your Christian life is full of the empowerment of the Holy Spirit, and there is regular, eternal fruit upon your branches.

Neal Leazer is an amazing Bible teacher in our local fellowship. He has a powerful website where you can investigate his teachings at *www.bornofspirit.net*. As I listened to one of his messages about the baptism of the Holy Spirit, a definition he provided resonated with me. He simply said, "The baptism of the Holy Spirit is power given you to represent your Lord more effectively."

Neal went on to give this visualization:

> Think of a house being built. The workers are using hammers and hand saws. The foreman comes on the job one day and brings a van-full of power tools. He passes out the power nailer and power saws. The workers begin using the power tools. The power tools simply help them get the job done more effectively and with greater ease and speed.

I love that picture. He went on to say, "The baptism of the Holy Spirit doesn't make you better than someone else. It just makes you better than you were before."

Thank you, Neal, for those insights.

In my forty-six years of loving God, I don't believe I've personally ever seen more controversy over any subject in the Scriptures as I have seen over the baptism of the Holy Spirit, the gift of tongues, and the other gifts of the Holy Spirit. Church splits have peppered history over beliefs about the very acts of God in both the early Church and the Church today (the baptism of the Holy Spirit and the Holy Spirit's ministry in and through believers).

It's my goal and heart to keep it simple here. I come to you with my insight based on the Word of God as I understand it (don't we all?), coupled with my personal experience. I will remain kind and respectful to those whose beliefs differ about this. I come to you in humility—not claiming to be a theologian but, instead, a simple disciple of Jesus Christ, who is ever learning and growing in the knowledge of His will and purposes for my life. We don't have to agree on everything, yet we can be kind, loving, and respectful about it all.

That, my friend, is so important to me.

So just *take a listen* here, and let me *stir the pot*, so to speak, and make you thirsty to dig deeper into the Word for yourself. If you don't agree with me, I remain respectful of that. I just know what God has done in my life, and I wish to share with you—with great joy—what I have discovered. Even if I can only cause you to study the Word of God to know more concerning the things of the Holy Spirit, I will be ever so happy about that.

In this chapter, I will provide Scripture and go through why I believe the baptism of the Holy Spirit is an important part of what God has for each one of us. For those of you who are a bit skeptical of this whole idea of the baptism of the Holy Spirit, I ask, "Why?"

Why wouldn't we want the empowerment to be our best in this dark world of depression and bondage? Why would God empower the early Church and not the end-time Church? Why wouldn't His gifts from the Holy Spirit be for us today? I can think of no good Scriptural reason for skepticism.

I would like to propose that a huge reason people don't want to believe in the baptism of the Holy Spirit is because they are afraid of the unknown or they have seen the abuse of the Holy Spirit's gifts and want nothing to do with them. I say, don't *throw the baby out with the bathwater.*

I will share why I believe the baptism of the Holy Spirit is a separate event from our salvation moment. In another place I will share my story of how I received the baptism at the age of fourteen (and it continues to benefit me to this day). Whether we ask for the baptism of the Holy Spirit at conversion or at another point in our walk, I believe it is an important step in our walk with God.

If the people who rubbed shoulders with Jesus every day for a few years needed to be baptized in the Holy Spirit, why wouldn't we benefit as well by being baptized in the Holy Spirit? I also believe the initial time we are baptized of the Holy Spirit isn't the only time we can ask for it. The Greek word for baptize is the word *baptizō*. It can mean "to dip repeatedly." I personally have asked for a fresh baptism in the Holy Spirit quite often on my journey with Him.

I desire regular and repeated absorption of God's power to walk above and not beneath my circumstances. I have experienced the fresh immersion of His power over and over again—helping me to not bow to fear, worry, panic, and dread. I am so very grateful for this beautiful promise of power to be a bright light and witness in my world for my Lord.

Let's look at the following portion of Scripture in Acts:

*And it happened, while Apollos was at Corinth, that Paul, having passed through the upper regions, came to Ephesus. And finding some disciples he said to them, "Did you receive the Holy Spirit when you believed?"*

*So they said to him, "We have not so much as heard whether there is a Holy Spirit."*

*And he said to them, "Into what then were you baptized?"*

*So they said, "Into John's baptism."*

*Then Paul said, "John indeed baptized with a baptism of repentance, saying to the people that they should believe on Him who would come after him, that is, on Christ Jesus."*

*When they heard this, they were baptized in the name of the Lord Jesus. And when Paul had laid hands on them, the Holy Spirit came upon them, and they spoke with tongues and prophesied. Now the men were about twelve in all.*

(Acts 19:1-7 NKJV)

Paul came across some disciples, and one of the first questions he asked them was, *"Did you receive the Holy Spirit when you believed?"* Paul found out they had been baptized only according to the baptism of John the Baptist. What followed was another water baptism—in the name of Jesus. And that was followed by the baptism of the Holy Spirit.

The way this passage reads, the Holy Spirit came upon them when Paul laid his hands on them for the specific purpose of them being baptized in the Holy Spirit immediately after Paul or his fellow evangelists baptized them in water. If the baptism of the Holy Spirit is automatically conferred upon people when they become a believer, why did Paul ask his question? Paul found some disciples who had never even heard of the Holy Spirit—interesting.

They needed to be water baptized into Jesus, and they needed the baptism of the Holy Spirit. They got the rest of what God wanted to give them. And they spoke in tongues and prophesied. According to this story, *water baptism* and *Holy Spirit baptism* are two separate, needed events in the life of a believer.

Let's turn to Acts chapter eight.

*Now when the apostles who were at Jerusalem heard that Samaria had received the word of God, they sent Peter and John to them, who, when they had come down, prayed for them that they might receive the Holy Spirit. For as yet He had fallen upon none of them. They had only been baptized in the name of the Lord Jesus. Then they laid hands on them, and they received the Holy Spirit.* (Acts 8:14-17 NKJV)

Feel free to read the whole chapter to get all of the fascinating story, but I want to focus on these verses.

These Samaritans had received the Word of God. They were born again and had been water baptized. Yet the Bible says that *"He [the Holy Spirit] had fallen upon none of them."* They were already temples of the Holy Spirit, yet they hadn't received the empowerment of the Holy Spirit.

The Jerusalem apostles sent Peter and John to Samaria. One of the things they made sure to do when they got there was lay hands on those who had been water baptized in Jesus so they would receive the Holy Spirit. Friend, I submit to you that if receiving the Holy Spirit's empowerment through the baptism of the Holy Spirit occurs automatically with the salvation experience, then why is this story in the Bible?

I heard David Wilkerson—founder of Teen Challenge—explain it like this once:

> Think of a glass filled with water. That is like when you are born again, and the Holy Spirit is inside you. Now put that glass in a bucket of water. This is immersion. This is what baptism means. The baptism of the Holy Spirit is the immersion of the Holy Spirit.

The Samaritans may or may not have spoken in tongues or prophesied after they received. We aren't told. But look at the following verses.

> *And when Simon saw that through the laying on of the apostles' hands the Holy Spirit was given, he offered them money, saying, "Give me this power also, that anyone on whom I lay hands may receive the Holy Spirit."* (Acts 8:18-19 NKJV)

This indicates that Simon saw something and wanted to be able to make happen what he saw.

In Acts, the general pattern was for people to receive the baptism of the Holy Spirit after believing and being baptized in water. And that is the pattern we most often see today. But the way Cornelius and his household were baptized in the Holy Spirit broke that pattern. They were baptized in the Holy Spirit when they got saved and before they were water baptized! Despite the pattern that occurred most often in Acts, and that we are more familiar with today, God is always perfectly within His rights to do things in whatever order He pleases!

I love that God is wild! He can't be captured and imprisoned by our earth-tethered thinking. Isn't it most important that people simply need to have an encounter with the living God? What if that means I get water baptized after I am Holy Spirit baptized? Or, what if I come up out of the water baptism speaking in tongues or prophesying? Can we just expand our thinking a bit and give God some breathing room?

It makes me smile as I think of this, but I wonder if God is ever saying He needs more space? How often do we put limitations on Him when He is possibly saying something like, "You are in my personal space. Please move aside so I can be free to do as I need to do."

I have a feeling I have gotten into the Lord's personal space at times and not given Him the room to move about as He likes.

Let's proceed on to read about Cornelius. I encourage you to read the whole chapter to get the full flavor of what God did.

*While Peter was still speaking these words, the Holy Spirit came on all who heard the message. The circumcised believers who had come with Peter were astonished that the gift of the Holy Spirit had been poured out even on Gentiles. For they heard them speaking in tongues and praising God.*

*Then Peter said, "Surely no one can stand in the way of their being baptized with water. They have received the Holy Spirit just as we have." So he ordered that they be baptized in the name of Jesus Christ. Then they asked Peter to stay with them for a few days.* (Acts 10:44-48)

Imagine Peter's thoughts as he was suddenly interrupted by an invasion of the Holy Spirit into the room. Peter was teaching, and suddenly he heard someone else talking. The Holy Spirit came upon them just as He had on the day of Pentecost. Those folks were just hungry for more. It was almost like the Holy Spirit said, "Ok, let's get this show on the road! I'm going to just arrive and not wait for Peter to finish his sermon. I cannot wait any longer to touch them!"

When you are truly, passionately hungry for what God has, there is no stopping Him from delivering all you are asking for in a sudden moment. In the fullness of time, God always comes.

In the next chapter in Acts, we read that Peter had gone to Jerusalem, and some circumcised believers confronted him about ministering to Cornelius and his household. They criticized Peter for even eating with Gentiles.

Peter then made his defense.

*As I began to speak, the Holy Spirit came on them as he had come on us at the beginning. Then I remembered what the Lord had said: "John baptized with water, but you will be baptized with the Holy Spirit." So if God gave them the same gift he gave us who believed in the Lord Jesus Christ, who was I to think that I could stand in God's way?*

*When they heard this, they had no further objections and praised God, saying, "So then, even to Gentiles God has granted repentance that leads to life."* (Acts 11:15-18)

That day at Cornelius' home, Peter gave God space. Good for Peter. He didn't know in the beginning what God was up to, yet he gave God space in his heart to be expanded. He learned that the baptism of the Holy Spirit and the fullness of the good-news message of the Kingdom of God was for Jews and Gentiles alike.

I can't think of one place in the Bible where God has limited His message of the Kingdom to anyone. All are invited, yet not all will accept the invitation. And all are invited to receive the baptism of the Holy Spirit, yet not all will accept it.

Did you know the disciples had the Holy Spirit before the day of Pentecost? John wrote that Jesus *"breathed on them and said, "Receive the Holy Spirit."* [67]So why did Jesus tell them to wait in Jerusalem for the promise if they already had the Holy Spirit? He said that because Pentecost wasn't about *receiving* the Holy Spirit. When Jesus breathed upon them to receive the indwelling of the Holy Spirit, I believe that was their born-again moment with God.

Jesus then later told them to wait for the *empowerment* of the Holy Spirit.

According to Scripture, this empowerment is a separate event in the believer's life, yet it is clear through Peter's experience at the house of Cornelius that the baptism of the Holy Spirit can happen at the same time as conversion to Christ. One thing I don't understand is, when Jesus breathed upon them and told them to receive the Holy Spirit, why didn't He just do all of it at that moment?

I was in a conversation about this one evening with my son-in-law (who is a pastor as well as a great theologian in my opinion). I love his insight. Of course we don't know if this is why, but here's a great thought and what he said:

> I personally wonder if Jesus was playing *softball* with them, as opposed to *hardball*. In other words, I wonder if He was simply taking it easy on them because they were already so overwhelmed by all the recent events—kind of like He

67 John 20:22.

was saying to them, "Look guys, catch your breath, process everything that's happened, and take some time to just breathe and rest. And then once you've rested a few days, I'm gonna dump out the whole deal on you." Obviously I don't know that's what was happening, but I do wonder.

So my point is, the disciples had the Holy Spirit before the day of Pentecost, yet according to Jesus, they still needed more. They weren't quite ready to start changing their world until they received everything.

Jesus was very insistent that they not start building the Church until they had received the power of the Holy Spirit. He clearly instructed them to wait in Jerusalem until they received the power (the promise).[68] You see, you can be a Christian and on your way to heaven, yet not have the empowerment of the Holy Spirit.

How do you think those early Christians would have done if they had not waited for what Jesus told them to wait for? I think they still would have been saved, but would they have been as powerful or influential? I'm not convinced they would have.

Peter was transformed from a man who denied Jesus to a man who proclaimed Jesus and helped to usher in 3,000 new converts in that single day.[69] I attribute that to the day of Pentecost and his baptism in the Holy Spirit.

I have never believed you have to *speak in tongues* to go to heaven. That simply isn't biblical thinking. But John the Baptist was clear in Matthew chapter three that there was a specific baptism that wasn't a water baptism. When we are baptized in the Holy Spirit and fire, there is a dimension of intimacy and empowerment that comes with it.

---

68 Luke 24:49; Acts 1:4.
69 Acts 2:41.

One thing that happens when one is baptized in the Holy Spirit is an amplification of what's already inside you. It's different for each person. One person's story will probably be different from the next, but all will be touched in one way or another.

The Church was born after the followers in the upper room were baptized in the Holy Spirit. It was as if the embers within them were fanned into flames when the great and mighty wind blew into them that day. As I see it, as the baptism of the Holy Spirit came, what was in them in seed form (what Jesus had already given to them) accelerated and amplified in such a way that they were carried to new dimensions of ministry and influence.

The once cowering, fearful disciples arose after Pentecost with a passion and vision for the kingdom of God in such a way that nearly all of them were willing to lose their lives in the name of Jesus as martyrs because of the way they shook the world. Will it be said of us we loved not our lives even unto death?[70] That's a great question, and it's worthy of our contemplation.

The Church was born on the day of Pentecost. The kingdom of God was preached with miracles, signs, and wonders following the proclamation of the gospel. Wow! It's so amazing to think we too can operate in such boldness and power.

> Behold, I send the Promise of My Father upon you; but tarry in the city of Jerusalem until you are endued with power from on high. (Luke 24:49 NKJV)

Let's look at the Greek word for power. It's the word *dü'-nä-mēs*. It speaks of mighty work, strength, miracle, or virtue. It denotes power for performing miracles and moral power for excellence of soul. It speaks of power resting on armies, forces, and hosts.

When you have been immersed in the Holy Spirit, there should be undeniable evidence the kingdom of God is all around you. And since "power" denotes *power for performing miracles,*

---

70 Revelation 12:11.

then clearly, miracles should be a regular occurrence in your life. You will also have boldness to love and share the message of the kingdom in a powerful way. You will step out and do things that don't come naturally for you, because God just put some "super" in your "natural!"

There will be regular occurrences of miracles, signs, and wonders. You will have the gift of tongues.[71] You will speak for God as His ambassador and tell people things that come straight from His heart. This, my friend, is what is available to you in an amplified measure when you are baptized in the Holy Spirit.

This is Christian living at its finest. Why? Because you will be able to represent your Lord to the world more effectively after being baptized in the Holy Spirit.

It really makes no sense to me when people say the experience of the baptism in the Holy Spirit was only for the early church. We have the same number of enemies they did. There are the same number of demons (possibly more) searching the earth looking for someone to devour. We have the same battles with sickness and emotional baggage the early Church had. Why wouldn't we need the same empowerment God gave them?

The truth is, we do.

# TONGUES (PRIVATE AND PUBLIC)

> *Therefore, my brothers and sisters, be eager to prophesy, and do not forbid speaking in tongues.* (1 Corinthians 14:39)

Some say the gift of tongues was only for the early Church. Others say it is of the devil. Then we have those who believe that it is just as relevant today as it was on the day of Pentecost. My position and belief based on Acts 2:39 is that the baptism of the

---

71  Mark 16:17-18; 1 Corinthians 14:15; Jude 20.

Holy Spirit and gift of tongues are still for all who will call upon the name of the Lord Jesus.

After telling His followers to go into the world with the message and demonstration of His kingdom, Jesus himself foretold what sorts of things to expect in the life of a believer. One of those things is about new tongues.

> And these signs will accompany those who believe: In my name they will drive out demons; they will speak in new tongues.
>
> (Mark 16:17)

Jesus never said that applied only to the early Church. Not only did Jesus never say that the gifts would cease, but—to the contrary—the language and context of Scripture actually seems to indicate in at least one passage that the gifts will continue until Jesus returns.

> For we know in part and we prophesy in part. But when that which is perfect has come, then that which is in part will be done away. When I was a child, I spoke as a child, I understood as a child, I thought as a child; but when I became a man, I put away childish things. For now we see in a mirror, dimly, but then face to face. Now I know in part, but then I shall know just as I also am known.     (1 Corinthians 13:9-12 NKJV)

Speaking in tongues is the scriptural evidence of one who has been baptized in the Holy Spirit. We have already established that in previous passages in this chapter. Next I would like to just talk specifically about tongues.

There are two types of tongues. There is the more personal prayer/worship language, and there is the gift of tongues meant for public meetings that require the gift of interpretation. The personal tongues that are used for prayer and worship are of great benefit to the believer.

*For if I pray in a tongue, my spirit prays, but my understanding is unfruitful. What is the conclusion then? I will pray with the spirit, and I will also pray with the understanding. I will sing with the spirit, and I will also sing with the understanding.*

(1 Corinthians 14:14-15 NKJV)

*But you, beloved, building yourselves up on your most holy faith, praying in the Holy Spirit, keep yourselves in the love of God, looking for the mercy of our Lord Jesus Christ unto eternal life.* (Jude 20-21 NKJV)

*One who speaks in a tongue edifies himself.*

(1 Corinthians 14:4a NASB)

This kind of tongues is used in private. Speaking in tongues is a beautiful way to pray as well as worship, especially when words fail. When one prays or sings in the Holy Spirit (praying or singing with tongues), there is a special edification and encouragement that comes with it. Every time I pray in the Holy Spirit I can testify to this truth.

For the past forty-plus years, this has been my testimony always. So many times life just got so difficult, yet when I prayed in tongues, heaviness lifted, and I could continue on in a much better place.

I asked a few amazing world-changers in my life—whose walks with God I highly respect—to share what the baptism of the Holy Spirit means to them personally. I share their thoughts with you now.

Anything Jesus says to wait for is certainly worth it. When He instructed the disciples in Acts one to wait for the gift of the Holy Spirit, they were not disappointed. This was true of me as well when I received the baptism of the Holy Spirit. Today, I can confidently say being filled with the Holy Spirit has granted me greater awareness of personal conviction and a deeper sensitivity to His voice for myself and in ministry for others. I know the baptism of the Holy Spirit is real beyond explanation, and He is absolutely worth the wait. He is the beautiful gift promised to each of us in the book of Acts. The Holy Spirit bears witness in man that we need a Savior, but the fullness, or baptism, of the Holy Spirit allows us to live out life in a deeper, richer manner. It's a little bit like a child who gets a 64-pack of crayons for school rather than the expected 24-pack—much more color!

—Pat, Ohio

Jesus healed the sick, raised the dead, and cast out demons. He performed miracles, like turning water into wine and walking on water. Jesus said, "Greater things than these you will do." We cannot do miracles or heal someone with our own power—we don't have power on our own. We have been given authority to do these things by Jesus. It is the Holy Spirit who gives us the power to do these things. When we are saved and do not ask the Holy Spirit into our lives, we are missing something. The ability to walk out the life of a Christian is given to us by the Holy Spirit. Otherwise we must depend on *religion* to get us there. Religion did not serve the Pharisees very well. If there is more to have, I want it. I want all that God has for me! I also want to give the Holy Spirit the honor given Him by the Father and Jesus! If it is important to them to honor the Holy Spirit, then it is certainly important for me to do also.

—Becki, California

For me, the importance of having the Holy Spirit active in my life is not having to depend on me! It's Christ in me. I have nothing to offer, but when He poured into me His Spirit, I became infused with Him and the power He gives me daily to walk in His power. When I face obstacles in my life and don't know where to turn, I'm reminded to pray in the Holy Spirit, because He knows exactly how to pray and what is needed. And every time, I am filled with peace. Now that's power!

—Gayla, Florida

The baptism of the Holy Spirit is essential for walking a Spirit-filled life. There are many things I could say in regards to how speaking in tongues is a necessity, but the major thing is that speaking in tongues actually facilitates the building up of our faith—that is, the essence of faith, not just the mindset. In the book of Jude, we are admonished to "build ourselves up on our most holy faith and pray in the Holy Spirit." In many situations, I have found speaking in tongues to be a major source of building up my faith in Christ Jesus. While I might be in the middle of what is seemly an impossible situation, as I begin to pray in the Holy Spirit my spirit starts declaring the mysteries of God. These declarations in the language of the Holy Spirit open the eyes of my faith to see the greatness and the majesty of God. My spirit joins with the Holy Spirit in speaking forth heaven's reality and strategies into the earthly circumstances that surround me. As my spirit and soul hear the confession of my mouth in tongues, my heart begins to enlarge in its faith-capacity, and I start to tangibly feel strengthened in the Holy Spirit. As I am strengthened in my faith in the greatness and goodness of God, my eyes become fixed on Jesus, who will lead me into victory. Faith comes by hearing and hearing by the Word of God (Romans 10:17). So we know God's Word opens our ears to hear, but the eyes of our faith are opened when we *hear* the Living Word. When I speak in tongues, not only can I feel the Holy Spirit, but I hear the language of the Holy Spirit as I speak it, and my faith is enlarged. Speaking in tongues isn't something done for show or theatrics. It is something that has led me—and I know will lead every believer—deeper into Jesus and into our Acts 1:8 inheritance of walking fully in the power of the Holy Spirit and moving into the "even greater works" that Jesus said we would do.

—Daneen, Oregon

The Blessing of Speaking in Tongues: The Apostle Paul said he thanked God he spoke in tongues more than most people. I simply thank God that He has enabled me to speak in tongues (other foreign languages and the languages of angels as well). I thank God that He has enabled me to speak directly to Him in communion and praise—both in words and in song—because as I release His Spirit to speak and sing through me, I am so incredibly, personally encouraged, and I literally feel my faith growing inside of me. How does this happen? It remains a mystery to my intellectual understanding, because this gift bypasses my mind. It is a matter of the Spirit. I have simply chosen to accept His gift to me by my small mustard seed of faith. I know as I have continued to both speak and sing in other tongues, my small mustard seed of faith has been steadily growing inside of me. Yes, it will always remain a mystery to my intellectual understanding as to how I feel strengthened in my faith as I speak and sing in other languages to God, but there remains no question my faith has been enlarged through this blessing in my spiritual life. *"But you, beloved, building yourselves up on your most holy faith, praying in the Holy Spirit . . ."* (Jude 1:20).

~Tami, Ohio

Finally, in the very words of Jesus, we are commanded to go into our world and preach the gospel to all. Jesus lays out specific signs that will accompany those who believe. Jesus spoke the following words to His beloved disciples and then left the earth. He left them behind, yet He continued working with them to confirm the Word through the accompanying signs He told them about.

And He continues to do it today through the blessed Holy Spirit—simply beautiful.

*And He said to them, "Go into all the world and preach the gospel to every creature. He who believes and is baptized will be saved; but he who does not believe will be condemned. And these signs will follow those who believe: In My name they will cast out demons; they will speak with new tongues; they will take up serpents; and if they drink anything deadly, it will by no means hurt them; they will lay hands on the sick, and they will recover."*

*So then, after the Lord had spoken to them, He was received up into heaven, and sat down at the right hand of God. And they went out and preached everywhere, the Lord working with them and confirming the word through the accompanying signs. Amen.* (Mark 16:15-20 NKJV)

## GOD'S WHISPER

Why do you fear what I have for you? One of the most contested gifts I want to give you is the baptism of my Holy Spirit. I tell you, hell trembles before every saint who has been truly baptized with my Holy Spirit. One who has been immersed in my Spirit will display boldness for my kingdom. The baptism of my Holy Spirit is a gift you truly need in the face of a demonic assault and its trappings. New abilities are placed upon you when the power comes. New breath and a refreshing blows through your heart as my wind's power settles upon and within you. When the wind comes, it blows upon the existing embers and brings forth an amplification of what resides within you that I have given you. It's like another layer of intimacy with me. It's a place not all are willing to go, yet all are invited. Fear will leave as you absorb my love. The Scriptures are clear, my heart is love, and you have need of this baptism to become more effective as a witness. Yes, you may witness without this baptism, yet with this baptism the amplification of Kingdom influence is multiplied. As you receive this holy immersion, you will not only speak in a new language, you will also prophesy. As you speak and declare on my behalf, you will open up worlds to others who are looking downward and missing what I have for them. How much of what I am offering do you want? The baptism of my Holy Spirit is offered to you daily. Daily immersion of my Spirit will bring daily wonders and empowerment to do exploits in the earth with me.

## PERSONAL APPLICATION

If you have been stirred in your heart and desire to ask Jesus to baptize you with the Holy Spirit, feel free to do so now. Here is a sample prayer to help you if you would like to receive the baptism of the Holy Spirit today. You can use this prayer if you like, or just talk to Jesus with your own words.

> Dear Jesus, I want everything you say I need to have. I desire to be empowered even more to be an effective witness in my world. I come to you now and say freely, "Baptize me with your Holy Spirit." I open my heart and ask you to loosen my tongue, that I may be immersed and receive the gift of tongues, just as you promised. Amen.

Dear one, if you just prayed to receive the baptism of the Holy Spirit, right now begin to open your mouth and let Him fill it. Begin to use your vocal chords and let the new sounds from heaven come through your voice. I'm so proud of you. If you don't receive tongues right away, don't be discouraged. Continue to ask. I believe it will come.

Now for my prayer:

> Father, I pray for this precious one who has just been baptized with your Holy Spirit. I thank you for the fresh dimension of your presence they have just entered into. Use them to advance your kingdom here on earth, as it is in heaven. Use them to cast out demons and heal the sick. Use them to make disciples as they go into all of their world. Let your glory swirl all around as they penetrate the darkness with your glorious light in Jesus' name. Amen.

## QUESTIONS TO PONDER

What comes to your mind when you hear the phrase speaking in tongues? Is it positive or negative? Can you back up your thoughts with Scripture?

Why do you think the baptism of the Holy Spirit has caused such division in the body of Christ?

In your opinion and knowledge of Scripture, is there any basis of truth to the thought that the baptism of the Holy Spirit was only for the early church?

Do you experience the power of the Holy Spirit on a regular basis? Why or why not?

Do you experience miracles, signs, and wonders regularly? Why or why not?

# The Refiner's Fire

## THE JOURNEY OF A PURE HEART

God's cleansing agent of fire will clean you up
and make you shine with His glory. You can't get this
kind of sparkling purity any other way.

---

*For He is like a refiner's fire and like launderer's soap [which removes impurities and uncleanness]. He will sit as a refiner and purifier of silver, and He will purify the sons of Levi [the priests].* (Malachi 3:2b-3a AMP)

Thomas Moore, a New York Times Bestselling Author, said in *Dark Nights of the Soul*, "You don't choose a dark night for yourself. It is given to you. Your job is to get close to it and sift it for gold."[72]

So as we explore the meaning of *the refiner's fire*, welcome the Holy Spirit now to teach you about this imminent purification

---

72 From *Dark Nights of the Soul: A Gide to Finding Your Way Through Life's Ordeals*, by Thomas Moore, published by Avery, 2005.

process for every believer in Jesus Christ. If we are to be transformed into His image, we will find ourselves in the heat of trials that are allowed to touch us for the purpose of purification.

When Jesus tells us we are the light of the world in Matthew chapter five,[73] the word *light* in the Greek is the word *phōs*. It denotes light emitted by a lamp—fire emitting light.

While I agree a *baptism of fire* means judgment on those who don't believe (the second death mentioned in Revelation 21:8), I also adhere to a belief that we as believers get to experience a refiner's fire while upon the earth for the purpose of purification and illumination. Therefore my focus in this chapter will be on the purification process of the believer in Jesus Christ in this life.

It's the pure in heart who get to see God, right?[74] We must allow Him to purify us in all ways. We must enter the furnace of the *Refiner* willingly—knowing that the temperature of the fire is under the total control of the Refiner himself.

Each work, motive, and agenda of our heart must pass through the fire in order that all we do comes from a pure heart. If our works on the earth are not made out of good material—the material we use to build on the good foundation that Christ and His apostles laid for us—they will burn up in the testing fires.

*Now if anyone builds on this foundation with gold, silver, precious stones, wood, hay, straw, each one's work will become clear; for the Day will declare it, because it will be revealed by fire; and the fire will test each one's work, of what sort it is. Each one's work will become clear; for the day will declare it, because it will be revealed by fire; and the fire will test each one's work, of what sort it is.* (1 Corinthians 3:12-13 NKJV)

---

73  Matthew 5:14.
74  "Blessed are the pure in heart, for they will see God" (Matthew 5:8).

As we give the Holy Spirit permission to refine us and the works we do, the light that comes from His indwelling work in us will produce a brightness to our lives that will manifest the illumination to others whom Jesus spoke of in Matthew five when He said that we were the light of the world.

In the King James Version of the Bible, according to the Blueletter Bible web site, the word fire is used in the Bible about 549 times.[75]

Fire is pretty spectacular if you think of it. There are many uses for it. I have listed just a few.

- Fire brings purification.
- Fire brings light.
- Fire cooks food.
- Fire brings warmth and pleasure.
- Fire destroys.
- Fire brings power.
- Fire can bring harm/injury if abused or not respected.

Let's flip this over into our walk with God.

Biblically, literal fire from God was often a type of judgment upon those who had rejected and rebelled against God. If you simply do an online search of this you will find the Bible is splattered with this type of fire.

As I meditated on this, I gleaned one thing. God will use either literal or spiritual fire brought upon every person who ever lived. Those who reject Jesus will enter into the lake of fire prepared for the devil and his angels. (Notice that the lake-of-fire judgment was prepared for the devil and his angels, not people. It's too bad others will join them there.)[76] But the fire I mostly

---

75 https://www.blueletterbible.org/search/search.cfm?Criteria=fire&t=KJV &ss=1#s=s_primary_0_1

76 "Then he will say to those on his left, 'Depart from me, you who are cursed, into the eternal fire prepared for the devil and his angels'" (Matthew 25:41).

want to talk about is the fire that we all go through while on this earth through the trials and tribulations we experience for the purpose of purification.

I think we can all probably say we have been immersed into a fiery testing from time to time. In my life, it might look like a prolonged season when Nathan doesn't have work, and the bills keep coming. There have been times when being married was just hard, and we weren't seeing eye to eye on this or that issue. Sometimes there were difficult relational problems within the family or with friends.

Times of testing and purification may also include chronic sickness or physical limitations. A time of refining simply means there are times when I enter into a place that could be called "Satan's hour"—as I heard Francis Frangipane say once. These are times when it seems justice and help feel far away.

There were also seasons in my journey with God when I had to return to home base, so to speak, and ask myself again, "What do I truly believe?"

There have been disappointments that I allowed to spiral me downward right into times of depression and discouragement. There also have been times when God hasn't answer a prayer in the way I thought He should have. At times God seemed so quiet, and my ability to hear Him seemed cut off. The types of *fire* I have just described could be part of the refiner's fire allowed by God to purify my heart.

So often I have emerged from these spiritual infernos strengthened, enlightened, and empowered. Even though these types of fires can be grueling, I look upon them as a gift. Pain is not the enemy. For the courageous of heart, pain is considered a gift.

Think of all the fiery furnaces that biblical characters went through. We have Job, who endured horrible loss. Remember Joseph, who was betrayed by his brothers and sold into slavery. We have the Apostle Paul, who suffered beatings and imprisonment for his faith.

Saint, the truth is, God is not the author of sickness and lack. We live in a fallen, sin-filled world. The god of this world (the devil) continually roams the earth, like a lion, looking for whom he may devour.[77] And you can depend on this: If God allows difficulties to come our way, He has plans to use them for our good—to teach us and refine our faith to allow us to see more clearly.

We, as children of God, are in need of purification. God wants us to see *Him*. The pure in heart shall see Him. When our hearts are full of distractions, unproductive thoughts, double mindedness, and the like, it takes a furnace of purification to bring the dross to the surface of our hearts—so God may skim it off and bring a greater purity in our lives.

Our lives should see a continual burning-off of what is not needed, so what is needed can remain and be strong. So when the enemy brings an attack against us, we are immediately exposed for who we truly are. We are *naked* in the flames of testing. God could remove any difficulty at any time, yet He doesn't always do that. I wonder how much He has kept from us?

Facing persecution and hardship, Paul and Barnabas said, *"We must go through many tribulations to enter the kingdom of God."* [78] The Greek word for tribulation is the word *thlipsis*. It speaks of things like affliction, trouble, anguish, or burden. I classify this verse as one speaking of the types of baptisms of fire that God said we needed.

The Psalmist wrote, *"Before I was afflicted I went astray, but now I obey your word."* [79] There is a type of paradox in Christian living.

---

77  1Peter 5:8.
78  Acts 14:22.
79  Psalm 119:67.

I need to give to receive and die to live. I must love my enemy and pray for those who mistreat me. Beauty comes out of ashes.

> *Then Job replied to the Lord: "I know that you can do all things; no purpose of yours can be thwarted. You asked, 'Who is this that obscures my plans without knowledge?' Surely I spoke of things I did not understand, things too wonderful for me to know. You said, 'Listen now, and I will speak; I will question you, and you shall answer me.' My ears had heard of you but now my eyes have seen you."* (Job 42:1-5)

Job basically had it all, lost it all, and then received it all back, and more. At the end of Job's story, he talks about seeing God where he hadn't seen Him before. Job gained something he didn't have before all of the tribulation he went through. Remember when we said earlier that the pure in heart shall see God? This is a perfect example of that. Job records that he had only heard of God before, but after the *testing by fire*, so to speak, he saw God—amazing.

I want to share with you a Puritan Prayer out of the book, *The Valley of Vision*:

## Lord, High And Holy, Meek And Lowly

Thou hast brought me to the valley of vision,
>    where I live in the depths but see thee in the heights;
>    hemmed in by mountains of sin I behold thy glory.
Let me learn by paradox
>    that the way down is the way up,
>    that to be low is to be high,
>    that the broken heart is the healed heart,
>    that the contrite spirit is the rejoicing spirit,
>    that the repenting soul is the victorious soul,
>    that to have nothing is to possess all,

that to bear the cross is to wear the crown,
that to give is to receive,
that the valley is the place of vision.
Lord, in the daytime stars can be seen from deepest wells,
and the deeper the wells the brighter thy stars shine;
Let me find thy light in my darkness,
thy life in my death,
thy joy in my sorrow,
thy grace in my sin,
thy riches in my poverty,
thy glory in my valley.[80]

Saint, Jesus not only wants to baptize you with His Holy Spirit, He wants to purify you in His refining fire. As you surrender to the immersion of God's inferno, you will find a life that compares with nothing on this earth. You will go into the holy furnace of God and emerge reflecting more and more the perfect image of the One who loves you to the core.

The refiner's fire equips your heart with a pureness that will burn off the scales to allow you see the One who calls you forward and onward in power, authority, and the sweet love of the Father.

The Holy Spirit's loving inferno will melt away the dross of that sin which so easily entangles you. His flaming candle will enlighten your darkness, giving you the ability to see where to put your foot next. The flaming embers of His love will bring desire and passion in your life so you will say with Jesus, *my food is to do the will of him who sent me.*[81]

The campfire of His presence brings peace, calmness, and reflection to your soul as you sit with Him and all His glory. Your

---

80 From *The Valley of Vision: A Collection of Puritan Prayers and Devotions,* by
Arthur Bennett (editor), published by The Banner of Truth Trust, 1975.
81 John 4:34.

chill-wearied heart will quickly be touched near His glory's fire. The flaming torch of God will be as a blinding light in the face of your adversary—bringing destruction upon the head of the one who hates you. The purification process Jesus brings will consume your surrendered heart in the face of challenge—causing the engine of your life to go full steam ahead!

There will also be a baptism of fire, so to speak, for those who reject Jesus. So either way, we all will be touched by *fire*, whether in this life or the life to come.

A soul surrendered to the refiner's fire will be a soul forever changed, purified, and fit for the Master's use. There will be a presence about you none can deny. Some say John Wesley stated, "Light yourself on fire with passion, and people will come from miles to watch you burn."

Other people say Wesley didn't say it. But regardless of who said it, it's a good word.

*For our God is a consuming fire.*      (Hebrews 12:29 KJV)

## GOD'S WHISPER

My refiner's fire is a holy experience. It is a necessary furnace for the one serious about my work in the earth. In the refining there is pain, testing, and challenge. Without the test, there is no passing over into the next realm of service unto me. Don't mistake my purification fires with an attack of your adversary. The surrendered one is safe in the fiery ordeal set by my hand. The scourging of the Holy Spirit will produce a pureness not obtained any other way. Go through your fiery ordeal, and as the dross of your life comes to the surface, I will take my skimming instrument and most gently and lovingly remove the dross. I will make you shine and reflect me by this baptism. It's the sorrow and the pain that positions you for the glory world. Suffering is a major component of this life. In eternity, there is no more pain, tears, or suffering—but not now. The intimate work I do in the dark places of despair and agony is eternal. I come into you and do the work as you choose to still yourself and remain aware that I am God. Hold still, dear one, and I will remove the infection of your soul. Stay quiet, my beloved, and I will make you shine as you emerge from your fiery ordeal. For the refiner's fire is a true gift to all who embrace this peculiar process of transformation.

## QUESTIONS TO PONDER

Have you ever gone through the refiner's fire? What spiritual benefits did you acquire because of it?

If Jesus learned obedience through the things He suffered (Hebrews 5:8), can you relate to learning obedience through anything you have suffered?

Why do you think it takes going through hard things to become transformed or purified?

# MY TESTIMONY

*For he says, "In the time of my favor I heard you, and in the day of salvation I helped you." I tell you, now is the time of God's favor, now is the day of salvation.* (2 Corinthians 6:2)

## SALVATION

The spring of 1971 was the season of my divine apprehension. I was just a child—nine years old. Brought up in the Church of Christ, which included attending church three times a week, I was no stranger to the regular hearing of the gospel message. Truly He does call, and woo, and bid. He comes in such a manner that even a child can comprehend the Father's desire that all be saved.

I remember the night like it was yesterday. The previous weeks I had been feeling a stirring in my soul. A burden, ache, or longing had been swirling around within me like a simmering pot. The drawing of my heart to God suddenly entered into a tipping point. That moment—that night—was the night Jesus came crashing down on my achy heart, gathered my lost soul into His arms, and seated me with Him at the Father's right hand.

All of my thoughts and desire for God culminated in that sweet, holy moment when heaven touched this nine-year-old little girl who had become ripe and ready to commit her life to the One who created her for His glory.

My sister, just six years old, was playing with marbles at the top of the steps. Just as I was going up the steps, all her marbles came tumbling and rolling down. At the same time, I was about to explode if I didn't invite Jesus into my heart.

She began to say, "Help me get the marbles!"

But I ignored her plea and turned around pretty oblivious to the marble chaos at hand. I went back down the steps to my mom, and crying, I explained to her how I needed to accept Jesus into my life and be water baptized.

My mom sat down, and with arms around me, she helped me do just that.

The evening of May 2, 1971 became a time of settling into the arms of my Savior forever! I was water baptized, and I emerged from the watery grave a new person in Christ. I remember going to school the following week with a newness of mind washing over me. I felt fresh, clean, and new.

Even at the age of nine, I knew I had just experienced an inner change. Life felt refreshing and invigorating. My life was never the same, and looking back on that moment, I count it the single most important decision of my entire life.

## THE BAPTISM OF THE HOLY SPIRIT

My next powerful encounter came on Saturday night, September 4th, 1976. Similar to the days leading up to my conversion, I had experienced a desire for more in my relationship with God. Our church was experiencing a struggle between those who believed in the baptism of the Holy Spirit—with the evidence of speaking in tongues and the relevance of all of the gifts of the Holy Spirit—and those who believed that it all ended with the New Testament apostles.

My interest was piqued when my best friend and her family began inviting me to meetings where the gifts of the Holy Spirit were in operation. "What is this? Why am I so attracted to this?" I began to ask a million (or so it seemed) questions throughout the summer of 1976. I began to study my Bible. I began to pray and ask God to show me.

I eventually landed in a place in my mind where I decided that I would ask God to give me this gift. I determined through Scripture study and conversations with others that I wanted this "baptism of the Holy Spirit." Even in the face of division, I determined that it was real and needed in my life.

On Labor Day weekend, 1976, I joined my best friend and her family and traveled to southern Ohio to Camp Prayer Unlimited. It was a campground where folks from all over gathered for the sheer purpose of worship, learning, and ministry. There was a large covered pavilion there where all the main sessions were held.

It was a weekend of powerful preaching and teaching God's Word. Those worship services simply captivated my hungry heart. As all those lovers of Jesus sang, it was almost as if I could hear the angels in heaven singing with us. I had never heard anything so beautiful. The voices of the people seemed to combine with a heavenly choir. I was captivated in worship and adoration of my Lord and Savior.

It was like tasting something I had never tasted before. It was heavenly and heavy with God's obvious presence, and I entered in and worshipped with my whole being.

Saturday night came, and as I listened to the teacher teach, my heart became ready to ask for the baptism of the Holy Spirit. The man sharing the word that night wasn't even talking about the baptism of the Holy Spirit. However, God was hovering and swirling all around my heart—lovingly calling and drawing me to the place of decision and reception of this marvelous gift.

I had studied God's Word and talked to many about it. Similar to the night of my conversion five years earlier, I felt I would burst if I didn't have this gift of the Holy Spirit that promised power to be a greater witness for Jesus! I had done my homework the previous months—asking questions and studying my Bible. I had become convinced that this was my next step in Christ.

That night, after the meeting, we received an invitation to go to a certain building to receive prayer for the baptism of the Holy Spirit. And so I went over to that room and proceeded to ask Jesus to baptize me with His Holy Spirit just as John the Baptist foretold in Matthew 3:11.

My fourteen-year-old self was immersed with power and fire that night—along with a joy that has never left my life! I remember going to bed that night overflowing with a fountain of joy like I'd never experienced. As I prayed, I surrendered my vocal cords to the Holy Spirit, and out came foreign words I had never spoken before. I had received the gift of tongues just as described in Scripture.[82]

I simply could not sleep that night. My mouth became the fountain of the living waters coming from my inner being.

*So what shall I do? I will pray with my spirit, but I will also pray with my understanding; I will sing with my spirit, but I will also sing with my understanding.*

(1 Corinthians 14:15)

To this day, forty-six years later, I use the gift of tongues as I pray and worship. It's been one of the most beautiful, amazing things ever! So often when English words fail in prayer or worship, I step over into that realm where my spirit is free to speak and express my heart.[83] When I speak in tongues, I have full assurance and faith that the Holy Spirit is speaking through me in prayers and songs that touch the heart of my heavenly Father.

*Out of his belly shall flow rivers of living water.*

(John 7:38b KJV)

---

82  Acts 2:4; Acts 19:6; Mark 16:17; 1 Corinthians 14:15; Acts 10:44-47.
83  "In the same way, the Spirit helps us in our weakness. We do not know what we ought to pray for, but the Spirit himself intercedes for us through wordless groans" (Romans 8:26).

I couldn't get enough of my Bible. I was in love with my heavenly Father in ways I never knew I could be! Boldness came into my life like I had never known before, and it turned this backward, shy, teenage girl into a girl who could share her faith with more power and boldness than ever before!

I received the baptism of the Holy Spirit accompanied by a new prayer language, which I use to this day! So often, as referred to in Jude verse twenty, I have used it to build up my faith. It's a mystery, but it's unshakable truth. For me, the decision to accept Jesus and follow Him, coupled with the baptism of the Holy Spirit, have been the rock-solid foundation of my walk with God. I believe after people are baptized in the Holy Spirit, all the good gifts, talents, and abilities God has given them are simply amplified. I am not better than anyone else, but I am better than I was.

I was baptized in the Holy Spirit at the beginning of ninth grade. My high school years were full of encouraging others to know Jesus. In eleventh grade I even had the privilege of baptizing a friend of mine in my farm pond. What a joy. What an honor!

I know the influence of God was on my life. Fellow students often confided in me, and God often gave me wisdom and counsel for them. I know His amazing power at work in me allowed me to be in the world yet be untainted by its effects. Drugs, alcohol, fornication, and all the familiar entrapments were not a temptation for me. I married about a year after my high school graduation and that's where the stories in this book began.

God has been so real to me over the years, and the power of the Holy Spirit I have experienced has always confirmed what I believe in Scripture. Having the gift of tongues has been such a reinforcement in my prayer life. I have learned the blessing of singing and praying with my understanding as well as the richness and power of singing and praying with the Spirit.

It has been a priceless gift to be able to open my mouth to pray or worship in the Spirit—a gift full of joy and encouragement.

The heartbeat of God in me is this:

Souls . . . souls . . . souls.

Just stop for the ones in front of you. Love them and touch them with the kindness of God. Just like Corrie Ten Boom said, "There is no pit so deep that His love is not deeper still."

It is the kindness of God that leads to repentance.[84]

We have got to learn the lessons the Holy Spirit is teaching us when we are engulfed in the flames of trouble! We have got to learn to hang on to the anchor of hope when the floods of trial and tribulation are swirling around calling for our death!

---

I conclude by telling you that the miracles of God continue in my life to this day!

This is an ever-unfolding story. I would do nothing different. My life in God has been the greatest adventure on earth! No thrill of the world can even touch the thrill of knowing Jesus Christ!

I was in a conversation with a young man the other day. He is struggling in his walk with God. He is struggling because he has never truly given God what He wants. I told him the *fun* he is engaging in is really *fake fun*. I invited him to step over the fence into true surrender to God and find an adventure of a lifetime. No fun in this world holds a candle to the fun I have in my adventures with God. He is my anchor, the lover of my soul, and the One whom I will see face to face one day when I cross over into eternity!

Christ's sheep hear His voice. Don't ever believe anything different. Are you His child? Then you should be hearing His voice regularly. I am one of His, and I do hear His voice.

---

84 "Or do you show contempt for the riches of his kindness, forbearance and patience, not realizing that God's kindness is intended to lead you to repentance?" (Romans 2:4).

I have been in prayer for another person when the sweet Holy Spirit shares with me a precious picture or word for them. And as I share it with them, they are in turn apprehended by His loving care on the spot. He gives me words for the weary and drinks of refreshing for the thirsty of heart. He whispers, "Pray for this one," and I do. And sometimes I discover they really needed that prayer in that very moment!

But most of all, I love it when He tells me He loves me and I am His.

I was brushing my teeth the other day. I was bent over at the sink, and the running water was creating a smiley face in the sink. At once, I recognized that peculiar image as God's smile upon my life. As we open our hearts to allow Him to express himself to us in all kinds of ways, the pleasure and joy of His heart for us will sometimes suddenly sideswipe us.

Here is my testimony to the world: I am not ashamed of the Gospel of Christ! For it is the power of God for those who are being saved! God so LOVED the world that *He gave*!

And so must I. I must love the world and give—just as He has. I must release people to be people and God to be God!

Jesus did only what He saw the Father doing, and He said only what He heard the Father saying. This is my goal. I want to study the workings of God in the earth. I want to be a continual student of His voice. I want to be draped in His power, so when I am faced with any demonic assault, I can chase off the enemy and cause him to run and flee in terror.

Mostly, though, I simply want to know Him intimately, intensely, and deeply. I want to make Him known and show off His glory!

My goal is to make history with my God. My desire is to see what He is doing in the earth and become one with it!

# CONCLUSION

You can have as much or as little of God as you want.

---

I have one more fun story to tell.

It was a Sunday morning—the day before I started to write this manuscript. We were at church. It was during worship, and one of the leaders in our church was sitting in front of us and suddenly turned around and asked if he could pray for us. I have learned to whip out my voice recorder when anyone wants to pray for me. I am accustomed to the Lord showing them things I possibly want to remember. On that occasion, I did just that.

Here is an excerpt from that Sunday morning impromptu prayer from our brother. He prayed and also told us this:

As I was worshipping I saw a picture of you guys. God was revealing to me you guys were like this tree. The tree had leaves, but no fruit. All of a sudden, all these butterflies just flapped their wings and flew away. I believe what God was telling me was that He was going to be bringing people into your life that are just going to make residence and just be on you. You guys are going to be developing them and they are going to be developed into butterflies. You are going to call them into their true calling. They are going to see you guys as just breathing life into them. They aren't going to know why they are attracted to you guys, but they're going to be coming from the left and the right. They are just going to make their home in your life. They may look like ugly caterpillars at first, and they don't have a lot of promise. Every time you speak to them you will be molding and molding them. And all of a sudden, the season came, and the entire tree . . . was just thousands and thousands of butterflies . . . just blossomed. And it was just the most beautiful thing.

I began writing this manuscript the next day. A couple of days later, I felt impressed to send the first few chapters to a good friend who lived in California. They lived right on the Pacific Coast with a view of the ocean from their balcony. She decided to take my manuscript out to her balcony and begin reading it. (Just a side note—I hadn't told her of our *butterfly word* yet.)

In her words, she told me:

I was sitting outside in my lawn chair, on my third floor patio, reading the first few chapters of your manuscript. I was completely covered with the Holy Spirit and chills as I read. I paused and looked up, and in the grass, down in the courtyard, there were butterflies—little white (I've never seen them before) butterflies. There were hundreds of them floating up out of the grass. They just kept coming. It was like bubbles rising in a glass when you pour a glass of soda. The bubbles come floating up from the bottom. That's what it was like. It was so ethereal. I've never seen white butterflies there before, and I've never seen them come out of the grass like that. They just kept coming and coming. I couldn't take my eyes away because I was afraid they would stop! It was magical, and I know that's not a good Christian word, but it was."

So there you have it! Another amazing God-story. Sometimes I just sit back and enjoy what God has just done. I have come to believe I don't always have to logically try to figure it out. Since I have asked God to astound and amaze me, when He does, I just smile, enjoy the moment, and say thanks! That's pretty much what I have done with this story.

Some things are just to be enjoyed—like a beautiful sunset, a child exploring and playing in the back yard, the sights and smells of the sea—you get the picture.

I hope you have been intrigued by our story.

My granddaughter Remi is one year old right now. One of my favorite things to do is to watch her explore in the yard. She is so intrigued with the simple details of the landscape. She loves to touch and taste and engage with dirt, stones, weeds, and sticks! Her attention is quickly drawn to a noisy bird singing her song. In the same way, I believe God finds pleasure as He watches us explore, study, and touch His truths.

I pray you dig into the Word of God for yourself the way my granddaughter explores the expanse of the back yard. I hope your walk with Jesus never becomes boring or mundane, or feels like you are simply going through the motions of religion.

It's okay if you don't believe some of my stories or disagree with my spiritual doctrine and thought. I know there will be the naysayers. I'm okay with that. But what I really hope to accomplish by telling our story is to make you hungry and thirsty for more, because there is always more!

In the words of Mark Batterson, lead pastor of National Community Church in Washington, D.C., "If you pray regularly, irregular things will happen on a regular basis."

Friend, seek friendship with the Lord. He is talking to you and loves to hear your voice in His throne room of grace. The holy dialogue in friendship between you and your Lord will escort you into wonders and adventures this world could never offer you.

*Jesus did many other thing as well. If every one of them were written down, I suppose that even the whole world would not have room for the books that would be written.*

(John 21:25)

# AND ONE MORE OF GOD'S WHISPERS

It's up to you. I have a whole bundle of surprises in storage just waiting to pass out to you. There are parts of me that aren't for you to understand on this side of eternity. There are mysteries, though, that I want you to unravel and learn. Did you know I thought of the hide and seek game first? I love to be sought out, and it's my joy to allow you to find me. True relationship is two-way. How boring to experience a one-sided conversation! Prayer is simply a conversation between me and you. Yes, I will speak to you. You've trained yourself to be one-sided in your conversations with me. Un-train yourself, dear one. Begin to put pauses in your prayers just to see if I am saying anything back. Learn to really converse with me. I will give you thoughts and ideas and wisdom as you listen. What I am most excited about is for you to hear me tell you how much I love you. Did you know I not only love you but I like you too? I do! My Holy Spirit is inside you. I'm that close. You are good at telling me what you are wanting and thinking, yet did you know I am good at telling you what I am wanting and thinking, too? I created you in my image, after all. So let's step it up a notch. What do you think? Are you ready for the *more*? I can't wait to hear your answer!

---

*Now to Him who is able to do exceedingly abundantly above all that we ask or think, according to the power that works in us, to Him be glory in the church by Christ Jesus to all generations, forever and ever. Amen.* (Ephesians 3:20-21 NKJV)

# ACKNOWLEDGEMENTS

I want to express my appreciation first and foremost to God the Father, God the Son, and God the Holy Spirit. Without the Trinity of God, the stories in this book and the encouragement that came with them would have never occurred.

Thank you, Nathan, my faithful friend and husband of over thirty-seven years. You helped me recount the stories of our journey together. Life with you has been so adventurous. Your example of steadfast faith and trust in God has encouraged me over and over again. These are your stories too. I love you with all my heart!

Thank you, Mom, for cheering me on and praying for us throughout the years of testing, trials, and miracles. Your faith is part of my foundation. Thank you. I love you, Mom!

Thank you, Emily and Jeff, Bethany and Rodney, and Levi and Rebecca for being my amazing "kids" nestled in the center of my heart. My heart beats for you, your children, and for all the generations of the Christopher household. Every one of you inspire me in so many ways.

Thank you, Carol McLeod, for your friendship and ministry partnership. Thank you for seeing something in me and being willing to go to bat for me! God has so evidently used you to open doors of ministry for me. Truly you have been the midwife for the birthing of this project!

Thank you, Suzi Wooldridge, for giving me an opportunity to be published through Bridge Logos. I have been overrun by the favor of God through you!

Thank you, Tami Hulse, for always stirring me up in the Word of God. I love our studies and dialogues around Scriptures. Your friendship continues on as a divine gift from God to my heart. Your encouragement, prayers, and editorial critique especially on this project, brought the help I so needed.

Thank you, Linda Baker, for your guidance, friendship, and prayers. Everyone needs a friend and spiritual mom in life like you.

Thank you, Cynthia Forry, daughter of my heart, for your love, friendship, and continual persevering spirit that inspires me over and over again. As we continue to cheer one another on, may we discover many incredible interventions yet to come from Him.

Thank you, Becki DeVore, for listening to my crazy stories and saying, "Yes, me too!" I so love you and the idea that God said we should be friends.

Thank you, Pam Mitchell, for your friendship and being a continual tailwind to me! Your prayers and encouragement to me in this project has been part of the wind in my sails!

Thank you, Tammy Stoltzfus, for your spiritual cheerleading! Thank you for your friendship! Thank you for knowing how to "rejoice with those who rejoice" in a very real way to my heart. Your excitement for me has touched me to the core.

Thank you, Linda Saunders, for your friendship and encouragement to me to pursue God's dreams. Your friendship and comradery is rare and precious to my heart.

Thank you, Marc Barnes, for your selfless giving of time and talent to produce my book video. You have such a gift.

Thank you, Leslie Barnes, for your dear friendship, fun personality, making me look good on production day, and your amazing heart for more of God.

Thank you, Christina DeCamp, for your labor of love and amazing photography skills! You have deeply blessed me.

Thank you, L. Edward Hazelbaker, for making this book shine and bringing the editorial expertise needed. I appreciate your critique, advice, theological challenge, and overall wisdom.

Thank you, Kent Jensen for getting this project ready for print. Your typesetting skills were the needed final polish. I am very pleased with your work.

And thank you to all who highly encouraged me about my first book, *Until the Day Breaks and the Shadows Flee*, and created a *wind* to help me set sail once again for this project.

# OTHER BOOKS BY CHRISTY CHRISTOPHER

*Until the Day Breaks and the Shadows Flee*
http://www.christineachristopher.com/

# CHRISTY IS AVAILABLE FOR SPEAKING ENGAGEMENTS

christineachristopher@gmail.com

https://www.facebook.com/Christy-Christopher-Christian-AuthorSpeaker-2089855587896541/

https://www.instagram.com/cchristopherauthor/

https://voiceoutofthewind.wordpress.com

NATHAN AND CHRISTY CHRISTOPHER
UNITED IN LIFE ON JUNE 6, 1981

# BEAUTY FROM ASHES
## Donna Sparks

In a transparent and powerful manner, the author reveals how the Lord took her from the ashes of a life devastated by failed relationships and destructive behavior to bring her into a beautiful and powerful relationship with Him. The author encourages others to allow the Lord to do the same for them.

Donna Sparks is an Assemblies of God evangelist who travels widely to speak at women's conferences and retreats. She lives in Tennessee.

www.story-of-grace.com

www.facebook.com/
donnasparksministries/

https://www.facebook.com/
AuthorDonnaSparks/

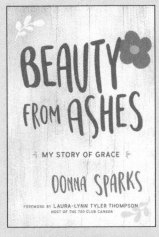

ISBN: 978-1-61036-252-8